Pocket
BARCELONA
TOP SIGHTS • LOCAL LIFE • MADE EASY

Anthony Ham

In This Book

QuickStart Guide

Your keys to understanding the city – we help you decide what to do and how to do it

Need to Know
Tips for a smooth trip

Neighbourhoods
What's where

Explore Barcelona

The best things to see and do, neighbourhood by neighbourhood

Top Sights
Make the most of your visit

Local Life
The insider's city

The Best of Barcelona

The city's highlights in handy lists to help you plan

Best Walks
See the city on foot

Barcelona's Best...
The best experiences

Survival Guide

Tips and tricks for a seamless, hassle-free city experience

Getting Around
Travel like a local

Essential Information
Including where to stay

Our selection of the city's best places to eat, drink and experience:

◎ **Sights**

✖ **Eating**

☺ **Drinking**

★ **Entertainment**

🔒 **Shopping**

These symbols give you the vital information for each listing:

☎ Telephone Numbers	🚸 Family-Friendly
⊙ Opening Hours	🐾 Pet-Friendly
P Parking	🚌 Bus
⊖ Nonsmoking	⛴ Ferry
@ Internet Access	Ⓜ Metro
🛜 Wi-Fi Access	Ⓢ Subway
🌱 Vegetarian Selection	🚡 Cable Car
📖 English-Language Menu	🚆 Train

Find each listing quickly on maps for each neighbourhood:

Bar Hemingway

16 ☺ Map p233, B2

Legend has it that Hemi
self, wielding a machine
rate this timber-pan
ered bar during
showpiece is a
en by Papa ar
town. Dress
s.com; Hôtel Rit
⊙6.30pm-2a

6 ◎ Plac

Lonely Planet's Barcelona

Lonely Planet Pocket Guides are designed to get you straight to the heart of the city.

Inside you'll find all the must-see sights, plus tips to make your visit to each one really memorable. We've split the city into easy-to-navigate neighbourhoods and provided clear maps so you'll find your way around with ease. Our expert authors have searched out the best of the city: walks, food, nightlife and shopping, to name a few. Because you want to explore, our 'Local Life' pages will take you to some of the most exciting areas to experience the real Barcelona.

And of course you'll find all the practical tips you need for a smooth trip: itineraries for short visits, how to get around, and how much to tip the guy who serves you a drink at the end of a long day's exploration.

It's your guarantee of a really great experience.

Our Promise

You can trust our travel information because Lonely Planet authors visit the places we write about, each and every edition. We never accept freebies for positive coverage, so you can rely on us to tell it like it is.

QuickStart Guide

Welcome to Barcelona

Barcelona could just be the coolest city on earth. Style conscious and always in fashion, this is a place where the avant-garde and the traditional collide daily with spectacular results. It's where Gaudí meets Gothic, where food is life in all its delicious complexity, and where the arts (including the art of having a good time) always take centre stage.

Diners sitting outdoors on Plaça Reial (p34)
BARBARA BOENSCH/IMAGEBROKER ©

Barcelona
Top Sights

La Sagrada Família (p104)

A temple as much to originality in architecture as to God, the recently consecrated La Sagrada Família is Gaudí's Modernista masterpiece and an extraordinary work in progress.

Park Güell (p110)

The playfulness of Gaudí's imagination takes flight in this park, which seems to spring from a child's fantasy of seriously weird structures and larger-than-life animal forms.

JEAN-PIERRE LESCOURRET/LONELY PLANET IMAGES ©

La Catedral (p28)

Barcelona's cathedral spans the centuries like a sombre and silent witness to the city's history. It's a towering edifice of singular and monumental beauty with a refined cloister inhabited by geese.

KRZYSZTOF DYDYNSKI/LONELY PLANET IMAGES ©

CHRIS MELLOR/LONELY PLANET IMAGES ©

La Rambla (p24)

Few pedestrian thoroughfares can rival La Rambla as it cuts a swath through old Barcelona and down to the shores of the Mediterranean. It's a canvas, a catwalk and a stage all in one.

Església de Santa Maria del Mar (p58)

This soaring Gothic church is a study in grace, harmony, symmetry and simplicity, and is a prime candidate for the title of our favourite traditional house of worship in the city.

Casa Batlló (p88)

Even Gaudí outdid himself with this fanciful apartment block: an astonishing confection of rippling balconies, coloured tiles, optical illusions and twisted chimney pots along Barcelona's grandest boulevard.

Museu Picasso (p56)

Pablo Picasso's enduring gift to the city he loved is this superb collection of the artist's early works – an intriguing study of Picasso's search for a style all his own. Above: *Las Meninas (Infanta Margarita María and Isabel de Velasco)* by Pablo Picasso (1957)

Mercat de la Boqueria (p44)

One of Europe's great produce markets, this is also the centrepiece of Barcelona's culinary culture. You'll find fine tapas bars and uniquely Catalan produce all under one roof.

Museu Nacional d'Art de Catalunya (p114)

Barcelona's finest art collection, this museum represents Venetian Renaissance masters, Romanesque treasure from the Catalan Pyrenees and a *Who's Who* of Catalan art.

La Pedrera (p86)

The fourth of Gaudí's unmissable Modernista gifts to the city, this apartment block is extraordinary both outside and within, a hallucinatory creation that only gets better the higher you climb.

Fundació Joan Miró (p118)

There is no finer or more comprehensive collection of Joan Miró's artistic endeavours than this museum. Miró is one of Barcelona's favourite sons and was a towering figure of 20th-century Catalan art.

Camp Nou & the Museu del FC Barcelona (p130)

In a city of temples and sacred turf, few rival the home of FC Barcelona for the passion it arouses. It's one of the greatest sporting stadiums on earth and a place of pilgrimage.

Barcelona Local Life

Insider tips to help you find the real city

If you're eager to experience Barcelona rather than merely tick off its signature attractions, we'll show you how the locals experience their city – traditional tapas bars and flea markets, Catalan traditional dances and local drinking holes that haven't changed in decades.

A Barri Gòtic Sunday (p30)

▶ Local markets
▶ Traditional dance

In the most heavily touristed part of the city, locals reclaim their *barrio* (neighbourhood) on Sundays. Join them at a mass in the 14th-century church where Gaudí was once arrested, then enjoy back-to-basics markets, visit icons of Catalan power and frequent timeless local eating haunts. In between, learn how to dance the *sardana*.

Revelling in El Raval (p46)

▶ Bastions of tradition
▶ Gritty streets

El Raval is the most diverse Barcelona neighbourhood, at once stylish and slightly louche in the manner of port cities down through the centuries. From the gentrifying streets of the north to the unreconstructed streets of the south, it's a journey through cultures and countercultures with detours to ageless Catalan classics en route.

Tapas & Bar-Hopping in El Born (p60)

▶ Tapas bars
▶ Drinking bars

So much of life in Barcelona as the locals experience it revolves around food, and El Born, a tight tangle of medieval streets near La Ribera's southern edge, is one of the best (and prettiest) places in town to go out for Catalan, Basque or broader Iberian tapas and drinks.

Sea & Seafood (p74)

▶ Fish restaurants
▶ Beaches

A bulwark of busy bars and fish restaurants where old-style cooking and fresh fish prevail, the old fisherfolk's district of La Barceloneta has held fast to its traditions. But the shiny new Barcelona has grabbed hold of surrounding beaches and marinas. They're two very different worlds in one city.

Evening drinks in El Born district (p60)

Shopping in the Quadrat d'Or (p90)

▶ Designer boutiques
▶ Gourmet shops

The Passeig de Gràcia is one of Europe's great shopping streets, a grand boulevard where the big names in fashion jostle for attention. But L'Eixample's genius is to throw up a whole culture of shopping, with the greatest affections reserved for local names in design, fashion and high-quality foodstuffs.

Village Life in Gràcia (p108)

▶ Old-style plazas
▶ Markets & bars

On the cusp of downtown Barcelona yet separate, Gràcia is a lovely mix of old and new, with markets, squares, bars and restaurants that date back decades alongside designer boutiques. And that's just how the locals like it – diverse, offbeat and a prime candidate for Barcelona's favourite village.

Other great places to experience the city like a local:

Planelles (p40)

La Colmena (p41)

Bar Pastis (p52)

El Passadís del Pep (p67)

La Botifarreria (p69)

La Cova Fumada (p81)

Carrer d'Enric Granados (p98)

Cafè del Centre (p100)

Sarrià (p135)

Barcelona
Day Planner

Day One

☀ Begin with Barcelona's standout sight, the otherworldly **La Sagrada Família** (p104), getting there early to avoid the queues. After a couple of hours (or more) acquiring a taste for Gaudí's flights of architectural fancy, head over to **La Pedrera** (p86) and **Casa Batlló** (p88). Browse for a while in **Vinçon** (p90) or shop for shoes in **Camper** (p102), then have a tapas lunch at **Tapaç 24** (p97).

☀ After lunch, stroll the length of **La Rambla** (p24), then dive into the narrow lanes of Barcelona's oldest quarter, the Barri Gòtic. Begin in **Plaça Reial** (p34), move on to the **Església de Santa Maria del Pi** (p34), then finish up at **La Catedral** (p28), but otherwise simply wander to get lost.

☾ As evening approaches, sample the best in Catalan tapas at **El Xampanyet** (p61), follow it up with some creative twists at **Bar del Pla** (p61), then move on to the enduringly popular **Cal Pep** (p61). Anywhere along **Passeig del Born** (p60) is great for night-time revelry, but our favourite perch is **La Vinya del Senyor** (p68).

Day Two

☀ Get an early start at the **Mercat de la Boqueria** (p44), wandering amid the market stalls and perhaps stopping for breakfast and a chat with Juan at **Bar Pinotxo** (p51). It's always worth checking out the exhibitions at the **Museu d'Art Contemporani de Barcelona** (MACBA; p49) and the **Centre de Cultura Contemporània de Barcelona** (CCCB; p49). Stop off for a hot chocolate at **Granja Viader** (p47) and lunch at **Ca L'Estevet** (p50).

☀ **Palau Güell** (p49) is a wonderful way to start the afternoon. After an hour there, head across the old city to the sublime **Església de Santa Maria del Mar** (p58) for an hour of quiet contemplation, followed by a couple of hours at the **Museu Picasso** (p56), one of Barcelona's most rewarding museums.

☾ **Agut** (p35) is a great old-city choice for a sit-down Catalan meal, or try **Pla de la Garsa** (p68). Otherwise, make an early tapas stop at **Bubó** (p61) or **La Llavor dels Orígens** (p67), and head for an uplifting live performance at the **Gran Teatre del Liceu** (p39).

Short on time?
We've arranged Barcelona's must-sees into these day-by-day itineraries to make sure you see the very best of the city in the time you have available.

Day Three

After an early morning stroll down La Rambla, drop off its southern end to **La Rambla de Mar** (p78), as a precursor to a morning by the sea. Pause for a lesson in Catalan history at the **Museu d'Història de Catalunya** (p78), then dive into the old fishing district of **La Barceloneta** (p74), emerging on the other side for a stroll along the beach. There are few finer lunch possibilities than the seafood restaurant **Suquet de l'Almirall** (p79).

For some of the best views in Barcelona, take the **Transbordador Aeri** (p78) cable car across to Montjuïc. Montjuïc's museums, vantage points and gardens are all worth exploring, but a couple of hours each at the marvellous **Fundació Joan Miró** (p118) and **Museu Nacional d'Art de Catalunya** (p114) will keep you busy all afternoon.

At the foot of the Montjuïc hill, **Quimet i Quimet** (p125) and **Tickets** (p126) are two of our favourite tapas bars in town. If it's summer, dance the night away in **La Terrrazza** (p127). If not, head for the Barri Gòtic and live music at **Jamboree** (p39).

Day Four

Use the morning to immerse yourself in two of Barcelona's most iconic (if very different) sights: the weird and utterly wonderful playground-like **Park Güell** (p110) where Gaudí's fertile imagination ran riot, and a stadium tour at the home of FC Barcelona, the **Camp Nou** (p130). Both are worth a couple of hours. Hop on the Metro and head across town for a meal at **Comerç 24** (p67).

Take a tour of the exceptional Modernista pile that is the **Palau de la Música Catalana** (p64) and spend some time soaking up the neighbourhood-market feel of the **Mercat de Santa Caterina** (p64). Another Metro ride takes you to L'Eixample's Passeig de Gràcia for some of Europe's best **shopping** (p90). Spend some much needed downtime taking L'Eixample's pulse at **Bar Velódromo** (p100).

A last night in Barcelona deserves something special: a splurge at the Michelin-starred **Cinc Sentits** (p99) or the Gaudí-decorated **Restaurant Casa Calvet** (p98). After a refined cocktail or two at **Dry Martini** (p100), take one last stroll down **La Rambla** (p24) to bid farewell to the city.

Need to Know

**For more information, see
Survival Guide (p171).**

Currency
Euro (€)

Language
Spanish (Castellano) and Catalan

Visas
Generally not required for stays of up to
90 days (not at all for members of EU or
Schengen countries). Some nationalities
need a Schengen visa.

Money
ATMs widely available. Credit cards
accepted in most hotels, restaurants
and shops.

Mobile Phones
Local SIM cards can be used in British/
European and Australian phones. US and
other travellers' phones need to be
set to roaming.

Time
Western European (GMT/UTC plus one hour,
or plus two hours during daylight savings).

Plugs & Adaptors
Plugs have two round pins; the
standard electrical current is 230V.

Tipping
Small change (€1 per person in restaurants)
and rounding up (in taxis) is usually sufficient.

 Before You Go

Your Daily Budget

Budget less than €100
▶ Dorm bed €15–20; *hostal* double €50–70
▶ Cheaper three-course lunch *menú del día*
▶ Plan sightseeing for free admission times

Midrange €100–200
▶ Midrange hotel double €75–150; book well
in advance and check online offers
▶ Lunch and/or dinner in decent restaurant
▶ Use discount cards to keep costs down

Top End more than €200
▶ Double room in top-end hotel from €150
▶ Fine dining for lunch and dinner

Useful Websites

Barcelona Turisme (www.barcelonaturisme
.com) The city's official tourism website.

Lonely Planet (www.lonelyplanet.com/
barcelona) Destination information, hotel
bookings, traveller forums and more.

Le Cool (lecool.com) Free, offbeat weekly
guide to what's happening in Barcelona.

Ruta del Modernisme (www.rutadelmodern
isme.com) Barcelona's Modernista heritage.

Advance Planning

Three months before Reserve your hotel
early to increase choice and reduce price;
weekends can book out months in advance.

One month before Book a table at Tickets
tapas bar (www.ticketsbar.es) or Cinc
Sentits restaurant (www.cincsentits.com).

One week before Book online entry to La
Sagrada Familia (www.sagradafamilia.org)
to avoid queues on arrival.

② Arriving in Barcelona

Most visitors arrive at Aeroport del Prat, 12km southwest of the city. Some carriers land at Aeroport de Girona–Costa Brava, 90km north of Barcelona. The main train station is Estació de Sants, 2.5km west of La Rambla.

✈ From Aeroport del Prat

Destination	Best Transport
Barri Gòtic	A1 Aerobús; Metro (line 3)
El Raval	A1 Aerobús; Metro (line 3)
La Ribera	A1 Aerobús; Metro (lines 1, 4)
La Barceloneta	A1 Aerobús; Metro (lines 1, 4)
L'Eixample	R2 Nord Train

✈ From Aeroport de Girona–Costa Brava

Destination	Best Transport
Barri Gòtic	Barcelona Bus; Metro (lines 1, 3)
El Raval	Barcelona Bus; Metro (lines 1, 3)
La Ribera	Barcelona Bus
La Barceloneta	Barcelona Bus; Metro (lines 1, 4)
L'Eixample	Barcelona Bus; Metro (lines 1, 3)

At the Airports

Aeroport del Prat Terminal 1 and 2 arrivals halls have ATMs and tourist information.

Aeroport de Girona–Costa Brava The baggage-claim and arrivals halls have ATMs.

③ Getting Around

Barcelona has an efficient and comprehensive public transport system. Apart from getting into town from the airport, the Metro (www.tmb.net) is the best way for getting around town. For some outlying areas, the Metro is supplemented by the FGC suburban rail network (www.fgc.net). Conveniently, both operate under the same ticketing system (as do city buses); it works out cheaper to purchase the 10-trip T-10 ticket (€8.25) rather than buying individual tickets.

Ⓜ Metro

Seven colour-coded Metro lines criss-cross central Barcelona. Metro stations circle the old city (the Barri Gòtic, El Raval and La Ribera), and the Metro leaves you on the perimeter of La Barceloneta. There are also stations all across L'Eixample.

🚆 FGC

The suburban rail network is particularly useful for Pedralbes, Sarrià and Gràcia. Stations in the town centre include Passeig de Gràcia and Plaça de Catalunya.

🚡 Funicular

A funicular railway (part of the Metro system) connects Paral·lel Metro station to the stations up the hill in Montjuïc; these additional stations are part of the Telefèric de Montjuïc, require separate tickets, and carry you to the summit. The Transbordador Aeri cable car connects La Barceloneta with Montjuïc.

Barcelona Neighbourhoods

Camp Nou, Pedralbes & Sarrià (p128)

Home to FC Barcelona, a 14th-century monastery, and Sarrià, Barcelona's loveliest village.

⊙ Top Sights

Camp Nou & the Museu del FC Barcelona

Park Güell ⊙

Worth a Trip

⊙ Top Sights

La Sagrada Família

Park Güell

La Sagrada Família ⊙

La Pedrera ⊙

Casa Batlló ⊙

Camp Nou & the Museu del FC Barcelona ⊙

La Rambla ⊙

Mercat de la Boqueria ⊙

Montjuïc & Poble Sec (p112)

Montjuïc is a world apart, with museums, a castle and Olympic relics. Nearby Poble Sec is a gastronomic hub.

⊙ Top Sights

Museu Nacional d'Art de Catalunya

Fundació Joan Miró

Museu Nacional d'Art de Catalunya ⊙

Fundació Joan Miró ⊙

Passeig de Gràcia & L'Eixample (p84)
Explore Modernista treasures, outstanding bars and restaurants, and a shopper's paradise to rival Paris.

◉ Top Sights

La Pedrera

Casa Batlló

La Ribera & Parc de la Ciutadella (p54)
La Ribera has a wonderful market, splendid architecture, plus El Born district – Barcelona's byword for cool.

◉ Top Sights

Museu Picasso

Església de Santa Maria del Mar

Barceloneta & the Beaches (p72)
Barcelona as it once was with an age-old culture of fishing, and an altogether shinier new beach culture.

Museu Picasso

◉

Església de Santa Maria del Mar

◉ **◉**

La Catedral

La Rambla & Barri Gòtic (p22)
Barcelona's old quarter combines famous La Rambla with narrow medieval streets and monumental buildings.

◉ Top Sights

La Rambla

La Catedral

El Raval (p42)
The former port district includes a fabulous market, bars and restaurants, stunning art galleries and an unlikely Gaudí confection.

◉ Top Sights

Mercat de la Boqueria

Explore

Barcelona

Worth a Trip

La Rambla de Mar (p78) at sunset
GTW/IMAGEBROKER ©

Explore

La Rambla & Barri Gòtic

One of the world's most celebrated thoroughfares, La Rambla is an essential Barcelona experience. Crouched along its eastern flank, the Barri Gòtic (Gothic Quarter), which dates back to Roman times, is one of Barcelona's most rewarding bastions of tradition, where ancient monuments overlook pretty public squares that provide breathing space amid the wonderful tangle of laneways.

The Sights in a Day

☼ Start your day as early as possible with a stroll down **La Rambla** (p24), then head for **La Catedral** (p28); the sooner you get here after its 8am opening time (Monday to Saturday) the better. Depending on how long you linger, you probably have time for a morning visit to the **Museu Frederic Marès** (p34), punctuated by a coffee in its cafe.

☼ After pre-lunch vermouth at **La Pineda** (p31) and lunch at **Els Quatre Gats** (p37), lose yourself in the labyrinth of the old quarter. The city's Roman heritage makes a fine way to focus your meanderings, stopping in the **Museu d'Història de Barcelona** (p34) and passing by the **Temple Romà d'August** (p35). And on no account miss the **Església de Santa Maria del Pi** (p34).

☾ As night falls, **Plaça Reial** (p34) is a fine place to begin your evening. After a meal at **Agut** (p35) or **Pla** (p35), catch some live music at **Jamboree** (p39) or **Gran Teatre del Liceu** (p39). Dance the night away at **New York** (p39), then end the day as you began: with a stroll down La Rambla.

For a local's day in the Barri Gòtic, see p30.

 Top Sights

La Rambla (p24)

La Catedral (p28)

🔍 **Local Life**

A Barri Gòtic Sunday (p30)

♥ **Best of Barcelona**

Catalan Food
La Pineda (p31)
Agut (p35)

Bars
Barcelona Pipa Club (p37)
Venus Delicatessen (p38)
Manchester (p38)

Live Jazz
Harlem Jazz Club (p39)
Jamboree (p39)

Getting There

Ⓜ **Metro** The Metro is the best option. Catalunya station (lines 1, 3, 6 and 7) sits at the top of La Rambla, Liceu (line 3) is at La Rambla's midpoint, while Jaume I (line 4) sits on the Barri Gòtic's eastern perimeter.

Ⓜ **Metro** Drassanes station (line 3) is at the waterfront end of La Rambla.

Top Sights
La Rambla

Everyone walks La Rambla during a Barcelona stay. In just a 1.25km strip you'll encounter bird stalls, flower stands, street performers, grand public buildings, a pungent produce market, pickpockets, prostitutes and a veritable United Nations of passers-by. More than anywhere else this is where the city's passion for life as performance finds daily expression, as a relentless tide of people courses down towards the Mediterranean in a beguiling counterpoint to the static charms of Gaudí's architectural treasures.

👁 Map p32, A3

Rambla de Canaletes to Rambla de Santa Monica

admission free

🕑24hr

Ⓜ Catalunya, Liceu & Drassanes

People fill lively La Rambla

Don't Miss

La Font de Canaletes

From Plaça de Catalunya, La Rambla unfurls down the hill to the southeast. Its first manifestation, La Rambla de Canaletes, is named after the pretty 19th-century, wrought-iron fountain La Font de Canaletes. Local legend has it that anyone who drinks from its waters will return to Barcelona. More prosaically, delirious football fans gather here to celebrate whenever FC Barcelona wins.

Bird Market

In keeping with its numerous contradictory impulses, La Rambla changes personality as it gains momentum down the hill. Stalls crowd in from the side as the name changes to La Rambla dels Estudis (Avenue of the Studies, officially) or La Rambla dels Ocells (Avenue of the Birds, unofficially) in Barcelona's bird market (under threat from ice-cream and pastry stands) where you'll be serenaded by birdsong.

Església de Betlem

A little further to the southeast, the early 18th-century **Església de Betlem** (La Rambla dels Estudis; ☉9am-2pm & 6-9pm; Ⓜ Liceu) was once the most splendid of Barcelona's few baroque offerings. Its exterior still makes a powerful impression, but arsonists destroyed much of the interior at the outset of the Spanish Civil War in 1936. Approaching Christmas, check out the *pessebres* (nativity scenes).

Flower Stalls

La Rambla's assault on the senses continues along La Rambla de Sant Josep (named after a now-nonexistent monastery), which extends from Carrer de la Portaferrissa to Plaça de la Boqueria.

☑ Top Tips

▸ Keep a close eye on your belongings at all times – pickpockets love La Rambla as much as tourists do.

▸ Take an early morning stroll and another late at night to sample La Rambla's many moods.

▸ Unless you're prepared to pay up to €10 for a beer, avoid the outdoor tables along the main thoroughfare.

▸ The balconies of the Museu de l'Eròtica have marvellous views of Mercat de la Boqueria's entrance.

✕ Take a Break

Want to sample Barcelona before the tourists arrived? Step into Cafè de L'Òpera (p37) for coffee and tapas.

If you're eager to experience the buzz of market life, pay a visit to Juan, one of Barcelona's great personalities, at Bar Pinotxo (p51).

For much of its length, La Rambla de les Flors (as it's popularly known) is lined with flower stalls, assailing passers-by with heady fragrances to accompany the gathering clamour.

Palau de la Virreina

The **Palau de la Virreina** (http://virreina centredelaimatge.bcn.cat; La Rambla de Sant Josep 99; admission free; ⊙noon-8pm Tue-Sun; Ⓜ Liceu) is a grand 18th-century rococo mansion set back ever so slightly from La Rambla's western border. It houses the Centre de la Imatge, an avant-garde exhibition space with rotating shows with a focus on cutting-edge photography.

Museu de l'Eròtica

Barcelona takes pride in being a pleasure centre and the **Museu de l'Eròtica** (www.erotica-museum.com; La Rambla de Sant Josep 96; adult €9, student & senior €8; ⊙9am-midnight; Ⓜ Liceu), a private collection devoted to sex through the ages, falls somewhere between titillation, tawdriness and art. Exhibits range from exquisite *Kama Sutra* illustrations to early porn movies, S&M apparatus and a 2m wooden penis.

Mosaïc de Miró

Opposite Museu de l'Eròtica lies one of Europe's greatest markets, the Mercat de la Boqueria (p44), and a little further along on Plaça de la Boqueria, just north of Liceu station, is your chance to walk on a Miró – the colourful Mosaïc de Miró in the pavement, which has one tile signed by the artist.

Gran Teatre del Liceu

Built in 1847, destroyed by fire in 1994 and resurrected five years later, Barcelona's grand operatic stage, the **Gran Teatre del Liceu** (www.liceubarcelona.cat; La Rambla dels Caputxins 51-59; admission with/without guide €9/4.20; ⊙11.30am-1pm, guided tour 10am; Ⓜ Liceu) launched the careers of José Carreras and Montserrat Caballé. The marble staircase, Saló dels Miralls (Hall of Mirrors) and 19th-century stalls are original.

Plaça Reial

One of the loveliest squares in all of Barcelona, Plaça Reial (p34) is where many visitors divert from La Rambla and enter the city's Gothic Quarter, which shadows La Rambla from start to finish. A nightlife hub, popular meeting point and home to some modest early Gaudí structures, the square is a place you'll want to linger.

Centre d'Art Santa Mònica

Further south La Rambla gets seedier, widens out and changes its name to La Rambla de Santa Mònica. This stretch is named after the Convent de Santa Mònica, a monastery converted into an art gallery and cultural centre, the **Centre d'Art Santa Mònica** (www. artssantamonica.cat; La Rambla de Santa Mònica 7; admission free; ⊙11am-9pm Tue-Sun; Ⓜ Drassanes).

Museu de Cera

In a lane off La Rambla's eastern side, Barcelona's wax museum **Museu de Cera** (www.museocerabcn.com; Passatge

Plaça Reial (p34)

de la Banca 7; adult/child €15/9; ⊙10am-10.30pm; Ⓜ Drassanes) has more than 300 wax figures of familiar faces from around the world. There's everything from displays of twisted medieval torture to figures of Prince Charles and Camilla.

Mirador a Colom

Centuries after he stumbled across the Americas, Columbus (Colón in Spanish, Colom in Catalan) was honoured with the **Mirador a Colom** (Pla del Portal de la Pau; lift adult/child €4/3; ⊙8.30am-8.30pm; Ⓜ Drassanes), a 60m-high monument built for the Universal Exhibition in 1888. Catch a lift to the top for a fine view down La Rambla.

Top Sights
La Catedral

For centuries the spiritual heart of Barcelona, La Catedral is a traditional counterweight to the avant-garde architectural flourishes of La Sagrada Família. Where Gaudí's flight of fancy speaks to the aspirations of a city intent on pushing the boundaries and embracing the future, Gothic La Catedral, at once lavish and sombre, anchors the city in its past. Begun in the late 13th century and not completed until six centuries later, the cathedral is Barcelona's history rendered in stone.

◉ Map p32, C3

Plaça de la Seu

admission €5 from 1-5pm Mon-Sat & 2-5pm Sun; free all other times

🕑8am-7.30pm Mon-Sat, 8am-8pm Sun

Ⓜ Jaume I

La Catedral's central nave

Don't Miss

Northwest Facade

From Plaça de la Seu, contemplate the richly decorated northwest facade. Although the cathedral was begun in 1298, the facade, based on a 1408 design, was not created until the 1870s. It reflects extravagant northern-European Gothic styles rather than the sparer Catalan version.

Sant Crist de Lepant

The main figure above the altar in the first chapel, to the right of the northwest entrance, is Sant Crist de Lepant. He was carried on the prow of the Spanish flagship at the Battle of Lepanto in 1571. It's said the figure acquired its odd stance by dodging an incoming cannonball.

Choir Stalls

In the heart of the main sanctuary – a soaring space divided into a central nave and two aisles by elegant, thin pillars – are the exquisitely sculpted, late-14th-century timber *coro* (choir stalls). The coats of arms belong to the Barcelona chapter of the Order of the Golden Fleece.

Crypt

The crypt beneath the main altar contains the remarkable alabaster tomb of the 4th-century Santa Eulàlia, one of Barcelona's patron saints; she suffered terrible tortures and death at the hands of the pagan Romans. Some of those gruesome tortures are depicted on the tomb.

Cloister

From the southwest transept, exit to the *claustre* (cloister), with its trees, fountains and geese (there have been geese here since medieval times). One of the chapels commemorates 930 priests, monks and nuns martyred in the Spanish Civil War.

☑ Top Tips

▶ Pay the €5 to visit in the afternoon; crowds are extraordinary during free admission periods.

▶ The €5 ticket also gives access to the choir stalls, Sala Capitular and the lift to the summit of the spire.

▶ Return at night to see the floodlit northwest facade.

▶ If visiting during the period of free entry, arrive at 8am before the tour buses arrive.

✘ Take a Break

No restaurants on Plaça de la Seu distinguish themselves, but the views from the outdoor tables are wonderful.

A short walk away to the southwest, La Granja (p31) is the perfect place to escape the crowds with great coffee or a scalding hot and thick hot chocolate.

Local Life
A Barri Gòtic Sunday

The Barri Gòtic can seem over-run by visitors at times, but it's on Sunday more than any other day that locals reclaim their neighbourhood, colonising the squares with small markets and frequenting places that few out-siders know about. Sunday is also the only day when two Catalan icons – the town hall and Catalan regional government – throw open their doors.

❶ Spiritual Start

Sunday mass remains an important part of life in the Barri Gòtic, so where better to begin than the 14th-century **Església de Sants Just i Pastor** (Plaça de Sant Just 5; ⊙mass 11am; Ⓜ Jaume I)? This Gothic church holds a special place in Catalan hearts: on 11 September 1924, Gaudí was arrested here for refusing to speak Spanish to a policeman.

2 Farmers & Painters

If it's the first or third Sunday of the month, make a beeline for Plaça del Pi and the **Farmers' Market** (⊙11am-2.30pm & 5-9.30pm), which draws vendors of fine cheeses, honeys and other artisan food products from around Catalonia. Around the corner, 50 local artists showcase their work in pretty **Plaça Sant Josep Oriol** (⊙11am-8pm Sat, 11am-2pm Sun).

3 Sardana

Catching a performance of *sardana*, the Catalan folk dance *par excellence*, is always a memorable event, at once an enjoyable spectacle and an important reassertion of Catalan identity. Your best chance is to turn up to Plaça Nova, next to La Catedral, at noon on Sundays when performances often take place.

4 Catalan Power

On Plaça de Sant Jaume, the **Palau de la Generalitat** (Plaça de Sant Jaume; www.gencat.cat; admission free; ⊙guided tours 10am-1pm 2nd & 4th weekend of month; Ⓜ Jaume I), the seat of Catalonia's regional government, was adapted from several Gothic mansions. The Saló de Sant Jordi (Hall of St George) is typical of the sumptuous interior. Visits must be booked online.

5 Town Hall Tour

Barcelona's town hall or **Ajuntament** (Plaça de Sant Jaume; admission free; ⊙10am-1.30pm Sun; Ⓜ Jaume I) has been the seat of city power since the 14th century. It has a Catalan Gothic side facade, while its spectacular interior features a majestic staircase and the splendidly restored Saló de Cent (Chamber of the One Hundred).

6 Coins & Stamps

While much of Barcelona is still sleeping off the excesses of the night before, dedicated collectors make their way to the **Coin & Stamp Market** (Plaça Reial; ⊙10am-2.30pm). Like all flea markets, it's always worth leafing through what's on offer in search of treasure, while some stallholders have branched out to sell a range of knick-knacks, both antique and otherwise.

7 Sunday Tapas

Going strong since 1930, **La Pineda** (Carrer del Pi 16; meals €20-25; ⊙9am-3pm & 6-10pm Mon-Sat, 9am-3pm Sun; Ⓜ Liceu) serves up a small range of tapas, from *jamón* (ham) to canned seafood in the finest Catalan tradition, all washed down with homemade vermouth. It hasn't changed in years and is a bastion of all that's good about the Barri Gòtic.

8 Chocolate con Churros

La Granja (Carrer dels Banys Nous 4; ⊙9.30am-1.30pm & 5-9.30pm Mon-Sat, 5-9.30pm Sun; Ⓜ Liceu) does some of the best coffee and thick hot chocolate in Barcelona. Buy your churros (*xurros* in Catalan; fried donut strips) a few doors up at No 8 and bring them here for an evening of dunking.

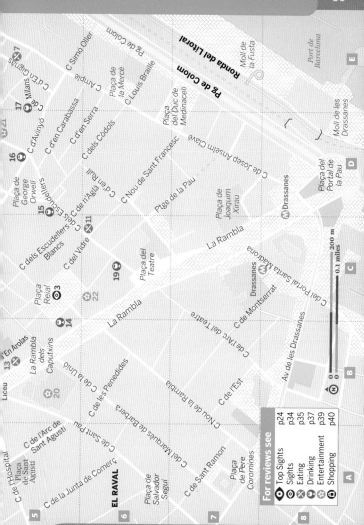

C de Simó Oller
C d'En Gignàs
C d'En Milans
C Ample
C d'Avinyó
C d'en Carabassa
C den Serra
C dels Còdols
C Nou de Sant Francesc
Pge de la Pau
La Rambla
C de Josep Anselm Clavé
Ptge de la Pau
Plaça de Joaquim Xirau
Plaça de la Mercè
C Louis Braille
Plaça del Duc de Medinaceli
Moll de la Fusta
Port de Barcelona
Moll de les Drassanes
Plaça del Portal de la Pau
Ronda del Litoral
Pg de Colom
Pg de Colom

Plaça de George Orwell
C dels Escudellers
C d'en Rull
C de n'Aglà
C del Vidre
C dels Escudellers Blancs
Escudellers
Plaça del Teatre
La Rambla
Plaça Reial
C de l'Arc del Teatre
C de Montserrat
C del Portal Santa Madrona
C de les Drassanes
Av de les Drassanes
Plaça de Sant Agustí

C d'En Arolas
La Rambla dels Caputxins
C de la Unió
C de les Penedides
C Nou de la Rambla
C de l'Est
C de Sant Ramon
Plaça de Pere Coromines
Liceu

C de l'Hospital
C de l'Arc de Sant Agustí
C de Sant Pau
C del Marquès de Barberà
EL RAVAL
C de la Junta de Comerç
Plaça de Salvador Seguí

Drassanes

200 m
0.1 miles

For reviews see

○ Top Sights	p24
◉ ○ ✕ ✪ Sights	p34
✕ Eating	p35
◆ Drinking	p37
✪ ✿ Entertainment	p39
⊞ Shopping	p40

Sights

Museu d'Història de Barcelona
MUSEUM

1 Map p32, D3

The 16th-century Casa Padellàs, which was shifted here stone by stone in the 1930s, sits atop the ancient Roman city of Barcino. Here you can descend into the remnants of the Roman town and stroll along glass ramps atop 2000-year-old streets. After Barcino, emerge into the buildings of the Palau Reial, the former royal palace. (www.museuhistoria.bcn. cat, in Catalan & Spanish; Carrer del Veguer; adult/child/senior €7/free/5, free 3-8pm Sun; ⏱10am-7pm Tue-Sat, 10am-8pm Sun; Jaume I)

Església de Santa Maria del Pi
CHURCH

2 Map p32, B4

This striking 14th-century church is a classic of Catalan Gothic, with an imposing facade, a wide interior and a single nave. The simple décor in the main sanctuary contrasts with the gilded chapels and exquisite stained-glass windows that bathe the interior in ethereal light. The beautiful rose window above its entrance is one of the world's largest. (Plaça del Pi; admission €3, free 9.30-11am & 6.15-8.30pm; ⏱9.30am-8.30pm Mon-Sat, 9.30am-2pm & 5-8.30pm Sun; Liceu)

Top Tip

Open on Monday

Many attractions shut their doors on Monday, but there are exceptions. Among the more enticing options are Park Güell (p110); Jardí Botànic (p125); La Catedral (p28); La Pedrera (p86); La Sagrada Família (p104); Mirador a Colom (p30); Museu de la Xocolata (p65); Museu del Futbol Club Barcelona (near Camp Nou, p130); Museu Marítim (p79); and Palau de la Música Catalana (p64).

Plaça Reial
SQUARE

3 Map p32, C5

By Spanish standards, Barcelona has relatively few public squares, but this 19th-century version is one of the city's prettiest and busiest. Carved out on the site of a former convent, it's home to neoclassical facades, palm trees and noisy restaurants and bars. The lamp posts were Gaudí's first (somewhat muted) commission in the big smoke. (Liceu)

Museu Frederic Marès
MUSEUM

4 Map p32, C2

This mind-boggling art collection was amassed by sculptor, traveller and hoarder extraordinaire Frederic Marès i Deulovol (1893–1991). He specialised in medieval Spanish sculpture, with a huge array of other knick-knacks including toy soldiers, cribs, scissors, tarot cards and some of his own sculptures. Snack in the shady courtyard cafe. (www.museumares.bcn.es; Plaça de Sant Iu 5-6; adult/child/concession €4.20/free/2.40; ⊙10am-7pm Tue-Sat, 11am-8pm Sun; ⓜJaume I)

Sinagoga Major SYNAGOGUE

 5 ⊙ Map p32, C3

The remains of what is mooted by some to be the Jewish ghetto's main medieval synagogue (not all archaeologists agree) were unearthed in the early 2000s. In the two rooms you can see remnants of Roman-era walls and some tanners' wells. (www.calldebarcelona.org; Carrer de Marlet 5; admission €2.50; ⊙10.30am-6pm Mon-Fri, 10.30am-3pm Sat-Sun; ⓜLiceu)

Temple Romà d'August RUIN

6 ⊙ Map p32, D3

Unremarkable from the outside, this courtyard houses the four soaring Corinthian columns of Barcelona's main Roman temple, built in the 1st century in the name of Caesar Augustus. Opening hours can be unreliable. (Carrer del Paradis 10; ⊙10am-7pm Tue-Sat, 10am-3pm Sun; ⓜJaume I)

Eating

Agut CATALAN €€

 7 ✖ Map p32, E5

This friendly family-run restaurant appeals to a sedate crowd that enjoys its old-school Catalan fare. Start with the sautéed frogs' legs or *escalivada*

(baked vegetables with anchovies) and move on to a range of meat and seafood mains; we liked the monkfish and crayfish in a romesco sauce. You'll hear a lot of Catalan here – a good sign. (Carrer d'En Gignàs 16; meals €30-40; ⊙lunch & dinner Tue-Sat, lunch Sun Sep-Jul; ⓜJaume I)

Pla FUSION €€

 8 ✖ Map p32, D4

The most chic choice in the Gothic quarter, Pla is a popular dining destination for young professionals. Chef Sergio Sánchez serves up wonderful dishes that, when we visited, included braised lamb in its own juice, light white-bean purée, glazed potatoes and leeks with a touch of thyme. The focus is modern Mediterranean, all served beneath a splendid medieval stone arch. (www.elpla.cat; Carrer de la Bellafila 5; meals €45-50; ⊙dinner; ⓜJaume I)

Top Tip

Roman Walls

The city's first architects of note were the Romans, who built a town here in the 1st century BC. Large relics of its 3rd- and 4th-century walls can still be seen in the Barri Gòtic, particularly at Plaça de Ramon Berenguer el Gran (Map p48, D2) and by the northern end of Carrer del Sotstinent Navarro.

Understand

Growth of a City

The Romans were, in the 1st century BC, the first to build a lasting settlement on the plain where Barcelona now sprawls. The nucleus of their city, known as Barcino, lay within defensive walls whose outline roughly traced what is now the Barri Gòtic, a more or less standard rectangular Roman town. The forum lay approximately where Plaça de Sant Jaume is now and the whole city covered little more than 10 hectares.

In the centuries that followed, settlements spread beyond the city walls. By the 13th and 14th centuries, Barcelona was the capital of a growing Mediterranean empire with a rapidly growing population. Its walls were pushed outwards to enclose what we now know as El Raval and La Ribera; La Rambla (which takes its name from a seasonal stream, or *raml* in Arabic) lay outside the city walls until the 14th century.

By the mid-19th century, Barcelona was again bursting at the seams. The road between Barcelona and the then village of Gràcia was lined with trees in the 1820s, giving birth to the Passeig de Gràcia with gardens and fields on either side. The medieval walls were knocked down by 1856, and in 1869 work began on L'Eixample (the Extension, or Enlargement) to fill the open country between Barcelona and Gràcia.

Designed by Ildefons Cerdà, L'Eixample took the form of a grid with diamond-shaped intersections, broken up with gardens and parks and grafted onto the northern edge of the old town, starting at what is now Plaça de Catalunya.

The plan was revolutionary; until then it had been illegal to build on the plains, the area being a military zone. Building continued well into the 20th century. Well-to-do families snapped up prime plots and raised fanciful buildings in the eclectic style of the Modernistas. With restrictions no longer in place, Barcelona grew exponentially, swallowing up towns such as Gràcia, Sant Martí, Sants and Sant Andreu.

Els Quatre Gats
CATALAN €€

9 🍴 Map p32, B1

Tiled walls, marble-top tables and wooden chairs set the scene for this haven of Catalan cooking. Expect dishes like roast shoulder of lamb, rabbit stew and salted cod served in a ceramic pot with chickpeas and spinach. At the turn of the 20th century, the bar was the hub of the Modernisme movement and Picasso held his first-ever exhibition here. (www.4gats.com; Carrer de Montsió 3; meals €25-30; ⏰1pm-1am; M Catalunya)

Cometacinc
FUSION €€

10 🍴 Map p32, E4

This atmospheric medieval-den-cum-designer-space produces an ever-changing menu of items that edges across culinary boundaries – tapas dominate the menu, with a strong base in deep Spain. The candlelit tables over two floors add a touch of romance and intimacy. (www.cometacinc.com; Carrer del Cometa 5; meals €30-40; ⏰6pm-1am; M Jaume I)

Los Caracoles
CATALAN €€

11 🍴 Map p32, C6

Los Caracoles has to be the Barri Gòtic's most picturesque restaurant. This tiled tavern has been serving up spit-roasted chickens and (as the name suggests) snails from the town of Vic, north of Barcelona, since 1835. It's all about atmosphere here and the photos of celebrity guests – everyone from Dalí to Charlton Heston – lining the walls distract a little from the at-times mediocre food. (www.loscaracoles.es; Carrer dels Escudellers 14; meals €30-35; ⏰1.15pm-midnight; M Drassanes)

Can Conesa
SANDWICHES €

12 🍴 Map p32, D3

For a quick bite, join the local workers from the ajuntament (town hall) and generalitat (regional government), who have been lining up here for the succulent *entrepans* (filled rolls), toasted sandwiches and other snacks since the 1950s. We especially like the 'Balaguer' – *butifarra* (local Catalan sausage) with Gouda. (www.conesaentrepans.com; Carrer de la Llibreteria 1; sandwiches €3-6.50, meals €30-35; ⏰8am-10.15pm Mon-Sat; M Jaume I)

Cafè de L'Òpera
CAFE €

13 🍴 Map p32, B5

This busy cafe is the most atmospheric on La Rambla. Bohemians and their buddies mingle with tourists beneath art-deco images of opera heroines etched into mirrors. The food is standard Spanish tapas – come here for the atmosphere. (La Rambla dels Caputxins 74; ⏰9am-3am; M Liceu)

Drinking

Barcelona Pipa Club
BAR

14 🍷 Map p32, B5

A former pipe-smokers' club, this is one of the most intriguing bars in the city – dim, laid-back and incurably cool. It's like someone's flat, with all sorts of interconnecting rooms and knick-knacks, most notably including the pipes after which the place is named. Generally it's for members only until 11pm. Buzz at the door and head two floors up. (Plaça Reial 3; ◷6pm-4am Sun-Thu, to 5am Fri & Sat; ⓜLiceu)

Marula Cafè

BAR

15 Map p32, D5

A fantastic place at the heart of the Barri Gòtic, Marula will transport you to the 1970s and the best in funk and soul. DJs occasionally slip in other tunes, from breakbeat to house, but this is all about the best in 'black music' – James Brown fans will think

---

> ☑ Top Tip
>
> ### Menú del Día
>
> One great way to cap prices on weekday lunches is to order the *menú del día,* which usually costs around €9 to €14. You'll be given a menu with five or six starters, the same number of mains and a handful of desserts – choose one from each category.
>
> The philosophy behind the *menú del día* is that during the working week few locals have time to go home for lunch. Taking a packed lunch is not the done thing, so the majority of people eat in restaurants and all-inclusive three-course meals are as close as they can get to eating home-style food without breaking the bank.

---

they've died and gone to heaven. (www.marulacafe.com, in Catalan & Spanish; Carrer dels Escudellers 49; ◷11pm-5am Sun-Thu, to 5.30am Fri & Sat; ⓜLiceu)

Venus Delicatessen

BAR, CAFE

16 🚇 Map p32, D5

A friendly neighbourhood bar that's a local favourite by day, Venus really starts to buzz after dark. Eclectic décor, casual service and a sense of being open to the world make this a great place to get your night going with a beer or first cocktail. (Carrer d'Avinyó 25; ◷noon-1am Mon-Wed, to 2am Thu-Sat; ⓜJaume I)

Manchester

BAR

17 🚇 Map p32, E5

This agreeable backstreet bar is all about New Order, the Smiths, Oasis and the Stone Roses. Inside, red is the predominant shade and cocktails the principal tipple. It's a fun mix that draws a strong British expat crowd and a few locals, and there are times when it can seem as if the 1990s haven't yet arrived. (☏663 071748; www.manchesterbar.com; Carrer de Milans 5; ◷7pm-2.30am Sun-Thu, to 3am Fri & Sat; ⓜJaume I or Drassanes)

Schilling

BAR, CAFE

18 🚇 Map p32, C4

No, it's not new, nor is it hidden away anywhere, and increasingly it's filled with out-of-towners rather than locals, but this gay-friendly favourite remains a great place to sip on a glass of wine or two before heading out into a more adventurous night. Grab a tiny round marble table if you can and ignore the somewhat frosty service. (Carrer de Ferran 23; 🕙10am-2.30am Mon-Thu, to 3am Fri & Sat, noon-2am Sun; Ⓜ Liceu)

New York
CLUB

19 🚇 Map p32, C6

Until the mid-1990s, this street was lined with dingy bars of ill repute. New York was one of them, but it's been reborn as a popular old-town club space attracting dancers aged 18 to 30. Friday night is best, with anything from reggae to Latin rhythms. (Carrer dels Escudellers 5; admission €10; 🕙midnight-6am Thu-Sun; Ⓜ Drassanes)

Entertainment

Gran Teatre del Liceu
OPERA

20 ⭐ Map p32, B5

Some good can come of disasters. Fire destroyed this old dame of opera in 1994, but the reconstruction has given Barcelona one of the most technologically advanced theatres in the world. It remains a fabulously plush setting for your favourite aria. (📞93 485 99 00; www.liceubarcelona.cat; La Rambla dels Caputxins 51-59; tickets €10-150; 🕙box office 2-8.30pm Mon-Fri; Ⓜ Liceu)

Harlem Jazz Club
LIVE MUSIC

21 ⭐ Map p32, D5

Deep in the Barri Gòtic, this smoky dive is the first stop for jazz aficion-

The ornate Gran Teatre del Liceu on La Rambla

ados. Sessions include traditional and contemporary jazz along with creative fusions from around the world, with deviations into flamenco, rock and funk; blues fans will love the Tuesday night jam sessions at 10.30pm. There are often two sessions per night with different musos. (www.harlemjazzclub.es; Carrer de la Comtessa de Sobradiel 8; admission €5-10; 🕙8pm-4am Tue-Thu & Sun, to 5am Fri & Sat; Ⓜ Jaume I or Drassanes)

Jamboree
LIVE MUSIC

22 ⭐ Map p32, C6

Jamboree has long brought joy to the jivers of Barcelona, with headline jazz and blues acts of the calibre of Chet Baker and Ella Fitzgerald. The tradition lives on. There are two hour-long

Q Local Life
Christmas Sweets

At Christmas specialist pastry stores fill with *turrón,* the traditional tooth-rotting holiday temptation. Essentially nougat, it comes in different varieties: softer blocks are *turrón de Valencia* and a harder version is *turrón de Gijón.* Check out stores such as **Planelles** (Map p32, A1; www.planellesdonat.com; Avigunda del Portal del Àngel 27; ⊙10am-9pm Mon-Sat, 4-9pm Sun; MCatalunya) which also does great ice creams and *orxata,* a summer tiger-nut drink from Valencia. The Planelles family started selling Christmas nougat in the 1850s.

jazz sets every night from 9pm and 11pm, after which the dance floor starts to fill with clubbers gyrating to hip-hop and flailing to funk. (☏93 319 17 89; www.masimas.com/jamboree; Plaça Reial 17; admission €12; ⊙8.30pm-5am Sun-Thu, 8.30pm-6am Fri & Sat; MLiceu)

Sala Tarantos   FLAMENCO

Since 1963 this basement locale has been the stage for some of the best flamenco to pass through or come out of Barcelona, though top-class acts are not a daily diet. For lower-grade stuff, a more pedestrian half-hour *tablao* (flamenco performance) takes place at 8.30pm, 9.30pm and 10.30pm. This place is at the same address as Jamboree (see 22 ⭐ Map p32, C6) and converts into a club later. (www.masimas.com/tarantos; Plaça Reial 17; admission from €8; ⊙8pm-6am Mon-Sat; MLiceu)

Shopping

Caelum   FOOD & DRINK

23 🔒 Map p32, B3

Carefully prepared sweets and other goods that have been the pride of Spanish convents through the centuries arrive here from all corners of Spain. Tempting traditional items include sticky marzipan and olive oil with thyme. Take a seat at a huddle of tables upstairs or head downstairs to what was once a medieval Jewish bathhouse. (Carrer de la Palla 8; ⊙10.30am-8.30pm Mon-Thu, 11am-11pm Fri & Sat, 11.30am-9pm Sun; MLiceu)

Gotham   ANTIQUES

24 🔒 Map p32, D4

This great retro shop specialises in furniture and decor (originals and reproductions) from the 1930s, '50s, '60s and '70s. Mosaic-covered tables, strangely curving seats that remind you of *Lost in Space,* and lurid lamps are only just the tip of the often-kitsch iceberg. (www.gotham-bcn.com; Carrer de Cervantes 7; ⊙11am-2pm & 5-8pm Mon-Fri, 11am-2pm Sat; MJaume I)

Ganiveteria
Roca   ACCESSORIES, HOMEWARES

25 🔒 Map p32, B4

If it needs to be cut, clipped, snipped, trimmed, shorn, shaved or cropped, you'll find the perfect implement at this classic gentlemen's shop, going strong since 1911. You'll also find a formidable range of bottle openers,

corkscrews and kitchen knives. (www.
ganiveteriaroca.es; Plaça del Pi 3; ⏰9.45am-
1.30pm & 4.15-8pm Mon-Fri, 10am-2pm &
5-8pm Sat; Ⓜ Liceu)

Escribà
FOOD & DRINK

26 🔒 Map p32, B4

Chocolates, dainty pastries and
mouth-watering cakes can be lapped
up behind the Modernista mosaic
facade here or taken away for private,
guilt-ridden consumption. This Barcelona favourite is owned by the Escribà
family, a name synonymous with
sinfully good sweet things. More than
that, it adds a touch of authenticity to
La Rambla. (www.escriba.es; La Rambla de
Sant Josep 83; ⏰8.30am-9pm; Ⓜ Liceu)

Formatgeria La Seu
FOOD & DRINK

27 🔒 Map p32, D3

This place is a gem. Dedicated to
artisan cheeses from all across Spain,
this small shop (on the site of Barcelona's first butter-making factory) is run
by the oh-so-knowledgeable Katherine
McLaughlin and is the antithesis of
mass production – she stocks only the
best from small-scale farmers and her
stock changes regularly. (www.formatgeria
laseu.com; Carrer de la Dagueria 16; ⏰10am-
2pm & 5-8pm Tue-Thu, 10am-3.30pm & 5-8pm
Fri & Sat, closed Aug; Ⓜ Jaume I)

La Manual Alpargatera
SHOES

28 🔒 Map p32, C4

The bright, white shopfront is a local
landmark. Everyone from the Pope to
Michael Douglas has ordered a pair of

espadrilles (rope-soled canvas shoes or
sandals) from this old-style store that
sees queues out the door as summer
draws near. The espadrilles come in a
range of shapes and colours and you'll
also find sun hats and bags. (www.
lamanual.net; Carrer d'Avinyó 7; ⏰9.30am-
1.30pm & 4.30-8pm Mon-Sat; Ⓜ Jaume I)

Cereria Subirà
ARTS & CRAFTS

29 🔒 Map p32, D3

Even if you're not interested in flicker-
ing flames, you'll be impressed by the
ornate decor here. Nobody can hold
a candle to these people in terms of
longevity – the Subirà name in wax
and wicks has been in demand since
1761, although it's only been at this
address since the 19th century. (Baixada
de la Llibreteria 7; ⏰9am-1.30pm & 4-7.30pm
Mon-Fri, 9am-1.30pm Sat; Ⓜ Jaume I)

🔍 Local Life
The Neighbourhood Pastry Shop

For almost 150 years **La Colmena**
(Map p32, D3; Plaça de l'Angel 12;
⏰9am-9pm; Ⓜ Jaume I), a sinfully
sweet pastry shop, has been serving up delicacies, from pine-nut-
encrusted panellets (sweet almond
cakes) to flavoured meringues,
detouring via all manner of Catalan
sweets en route. It also does lovely
croissants and the even better,
feather-light ensaïmadas (soft,
sweet buns topped with powdered
sugar) from Mallorca.

Explore

El Raval

El Raval, lined up along the western side of La Rambla, boasts the Mercat de la Boqueria and much more besides. In the north, two stunning centres for contemporary arts and designer eateries showcase the city's future. Away to the south, old-style Catalan restaurants and all the gritty detail of Barcelona's port-city past tell a very different story. In short, El Raval is Barcelona in a microcosm.

The Sights in a Day

☀ The **Mercat de la Boqueria** (p44) ranks among the most enduring of Barcelona institutions and it's at its best in the morning; we recommend at least a couple of hours here. Leave behind the cries of fishmongers and make your way to the **Museu d'Art Contemporani de Barcelona** (MACBA; p49) to sample the cutting edge of contemporary art.

☀ After a pre-lunch *aperitivo* at **Elisabets** (p47) and a sit-down lunch at **Ca L'Estevet** (p50), return for an exhibition or two at the **Centre de Cultura Contemporània de Barcelona** (CCCB; p49). Head south, via Barcelona's favourite milk bar, **Granja Viader** (p47), to the old city's only Gaudí masterpiece, **Palau Güell** (p49), then continue on to **Església de Sant Pau del Camp** (p47), one of Barcelona's most tranquil churches.

☽ A wine at **Bodega 1800** (p50) is a fine way to kick off the night, followed by dinner at sophisticated **Biblioteca** (p50). To experience El Raval's gritty underbelly, try **Bar Marsella** (p47), but spend most of your night in enduring *barrio* (neighbourhood) classics: **Casa Almirall** (p52), **London Bar** (p52) or **Boadas** (p51).

For a local's day out in El Raval, see p46.

◉ Top Sights

Mercat de la Boqueria (p44)

◯ Local Life

Revelling in El Raval (p46)

💜 Best of Barcelona

Contemporary Art & Architecture

Museu d'Art Contemporani de Barcelona (MACBA; p49)

Centre de Cultura Contemporània de Barcelona (CCCB; p49)

Palau Güell (p49)

Catalan Cooking

Ca l'Estevet (p50)

Bodega 1800 (p50)

L'Havana (p51)

Mercat de la Boqueria (p44)

Elisabets (p47)

Getting There

Ⓜ **Metro** Your best transport option. Catalunya (lines 1, 3, 6 and 7) and Universitat (lines 1 and 2) sit at the neighbourhood's northern end, while Liceu (line 3) occupies the midpoint, on La Rambla to the east.

Ⓜ **Metro** Drassanes (line 3), Paral·lel (lines 2 and 3) and Sant Antoni (line 2) are good for southern El Raval.

Top Sights
Mercat de la Boqueria

Barcelona's most agreeable sensory experience is found at its central market. Completed in 1914 with a Modernisme-influenced design, this is one Barcelona landmark where the architecture is overshadowed by what lies within – the freshest produce from around Spain, the evocative starting point of many a memorable Barcelona meal, and a hum of activity unlike anywhere else in the city. Wander to get lost. Marvel at the sheer variety. And then sit back to watch from a bar stool.

◉ Map p48, C3

www.boqueria.info

La Rambla de Sant Josep 91

🕗 8am-8.30pm Mon-Sat

Ⓜ Liceu

Fruit stall at Mercat de la Boqueria

Don't Miss

Fish Market

While stalls aimed at tourists make tentative inroads, the fish market in the market's geographical centre is the guardian of tradition. Razor clams and red prawns, salmon, sea bass and swordfish, it's all as fresh as when it was caught; so much so that there's scarcely a fishy aroma to inhale. Barcelona's love affair with fish and seafood starts here.

Juan at Bar Pinotxo

As one respected Barcelona food critic described him, Juan is 'the true spirit of the market'. Head barman at Bar Pinotxo (p51) for more than four decades, resplendent in waistcoat and bow tie, and unfailingly warm in many languages and none, he cajoles his staff, greets passers-by and announces the daily specials in the finest Barcelona tradition of food as performance.

El Llar del Pernil

The family-run **El Llar del Pernil** (⊙8am-4pm Tue-Thu, to 5pm Fri & Sat) is our pick of the numerous purveyors of *jamón* (cured Spanish-style ham; *pernil* in Catalan) scattered around the market. Stall owner Joan knows his *jamón,* cheerfully regaling passers-by with lessons in the dark arts of cured meats as he cuts another *jamón* wafer-thin and hands it over to try.

El Quim

The food at **El Quim** (⊙7am-4pm Tue-Thu, to 5pm Fri & Sat), buried in the heart of the market, is as fresh as the market produce. It offers a dazzling array of dishes, but does particularly wonderful things with eggs: *tortilla de patatas* (Spanish omelette), fried eggs with squid, or with foie gras... Pull up a stool.

☑ Top Tips

▶ Many stalls, including most of those selling fish, are closed on Monday.

▶ A handful of stalls open on Sunday but most of the market is closed.

▶ The market's stallholders are among the world's most photographed – ask permission before taking pictures and where possible buy something from their stall.

▶ Gather food from your favourite stalls with a picnic in mind – having a foodie purpose brings a whole new dimension to your market experience.

✕ Take a Break

For market-fresh food and some of the market's best cooking, pull up a stool at El Quim.

To soak up the clamour from a front-row vantage point, stop by Bar Pinotxo (p51).

Local Life
Revelling in El Raval

El Raval is a neighbour-hood whose contradictory impulses are legion. This journey through the local life of the *barrio* takes you from haunts beloved by the savvy young profes-sionals moving into the area to gritty streetscapes and one-time slums frequented by Barcelona's immigrants and street-walkers. En route, we stop at places that, unlike the rest of the neighbourhood, haven't changed in decades.

❶ A Neighbourhood Square

For a slice of local life, the Plaça de Vicenç Martorell is difficult to beat. It's where the locals come to play with their kids or read the news-papers over a coffee or wine at **Bar Kasparo** (Plaça de Vicenç Martorell 4; ⏰9am-10pm; **M**Catalunya). Just a short hop from La Rambla, this is Barcelona as locals live it.

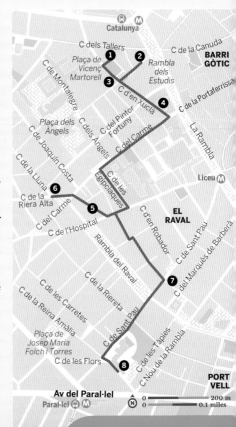

❷ A Musical Street

Seemingly every shop along Carrer dels Tallers has a musical bent, from purveyors of flamenco and other guitars to record and CD stores. Around the corner, **Etnomusic** (www. etnomusic.com; Carrer del Bonsuccés 6; ⏰5-8pm Mon, 11am-2pm & 5-8pm Tue-Sat; MCatalunya) is a great little store with music from all corners of the globe.

❸ Home-Style Cooking

Northern El Raval is rapidly gentrifying, but places like **Elisabets** (Carrer d'Elisabets 2-4; ⏰7.30am-11pm Mon-Thu, 7.30am-2am Fri & Sat, closed Aug; MCatalunya) hold firm. The walls are lined with old radio sets, the lunch menu varies daily and the best orders are an *entrepan* (filled roll) or *fuet de Vic* (cold Catalan sausage from Vic).

❹ Homemade Hot Chocolate

The fifth generation of its founding family runs **Granja Viader** (Carrer d'en Xuclà 4; ⏰5-8.30pm Mon, 9am-1.30pm & 5-8.30pm Tue-Sat; MCatalunya), an atmospheric milk bar and cafe established in 1873. This place invented *cacaolat*, the chocolate-and-skimmed-milk drink now popular all over Spain. Try a cup of homemade hot chocolate and whipped cream (ask for a *suís*).

❺ Preloved Shopping

Looking for fashion bargains that are perfect for passing unnoticed in this 'hood? In little more than 100m along Carrer de la Riera Baixa, from Carrer de l'Hospital to Carrer del Carme, you'll find nearly a dozen clothes shops, mostly selling second hand. For some variety, a couple of second-hand record stores also jostle for space.

❻ El Raval in a Nutshell

A tiny place with a half-dozen tables, **Mama i Teca** (Carrer de la Lluna 4; ⏰lunch & dinner Sun-Mon & Wed-Fri, dinner Sat; MSant Antoni) is more a lifestyle than a restaurant. The setting is a multicultural and often rowdy street deep in El Raval; the food is resolutely Catalan and served without rush. If you're not hungry, order a *cava* (Catalan sparkling wine).

❼ The Underbelly

Bar Marsella (Carrer de Sant Pau 65; ⏰10pm-2am Mon-Thu, to 3am Fri & Sat; MLiceu) opened in 1820 and has barely changed since – assorted chandeliers, tiles and mirrors decorate its one rambunctious room. Order an absinthe. Outside, Carrer de Sant Ramon is home to an international brigade of streetwalkers, drug dealers and old men discussing football.

❽ A Final Resting Place

Barcelona's oldest church, **Església de Sant Pau del Camp** (Carrer de Sant Pau 101; ⏰10am-1.30pm & 4-7.30pm Mon-Sat; MParal·lel) was founded by monks in the 9th century. It has some wonderful Visigothic sculptural decoration on its doorway and a serene air. The cloister is the best example of Romanesque architecture in the city.

Universitat de Barcelona

Catalunya

Urquinaona

Gran Via de les Corts Catalanes

Plaça de Catalunya

LA RIBERA

Ronda de la Universitat

C de Fontanella

C d'Estruc

C Comtal

Via Laietana

Plaça d'Anton Maura

C de Bergara

Catalunya

C de Montsió

Plaça Universitat

C de Pelai

Rambla de Canaletes

C de Santa Anna

BARRI GÒTIC

Pla de la Seu

Plaça de la Universitat

C dels Tallers

C de la Canuda

Plaça Nova

Plaça de Goya

CCCB

19

Plaça de Vicenç Martorell

11

Rambla dels Estudis

Plaça de la Vila de Madrid

C de la Portaferrissa

C de la Palla

C del Bisbe

Plaça de Sant Jaume

3

C de Montalegre

20

C del Pintor Fortuny

6

C de Valldonzella

C del Tigre

17

2

MACBA

Plaça dels Àngels

22

C dels Àngels

La Rambla de Sant Josep

Plaça de Sant Josep Oriol

C de la Boqueria

C del Call

CIUTAT VELLA

21

7

Mercat de la Boqueria

8

C de Ferran

C d'Avinyó

12

C de Joaquín Costa

9

C de Lleó

C de la Lluna

4 Antic Hospital de la Santa Creu

Liceu

La Rambla

Plaça Reial

Plaça del Pes de la Palla

14

16

18

C de la Riera Alta

C del Carme

La Rambla dels Caputxins

C dels Escudellers

Plaça del Padró

C de l'Hospital

Rambla del Raval

EL RAVAL

C de la Junta de Comerç

C de Sant Pau

1

Palau Güell

Plaça del Teatre

Sant Antoni

Ronda de Sant Pau

C de la Cera

C de l'Aurora

C de la Riereta

Plaça de Salvador Seguí

C del Marquès de Barberà

13

La Rambla de Santa Mònica

15

SANT ANTONI

C de les Carretes

C de la Reina Amàlia

10

Drassanes

Plaça de Josep Maria Folch i Torres

C de les Tàpies

C Nou de la Rambla

C de l'Om

Av de les Drassanes

C de l'Arc del Teatre

Plaça del Portal de la Pau

PORT VELL

Paral·lel

Av del Paral·lel

Parc de les Tres Xemeneies

0   200 m
0   0.1 miles

Sights

Palau Güell
NOTABLE BUILDING

1 Map p48, D4

With this commission for wealthy patron Eusebi Güell, Antoni Gaudí first showed what he was capable of. Sombre compared with his later whims, it's still a characteristic riot of styles (Gothic, Islamic, art nouveau) and materials. The 2nd-floor main hall is a parabolic pyramid, while the roof is a Gaudían carnival of ceramic colour and fanciful design. (www.palauguell.cat; Carrer Nou de la Rambla 3-5; adult/child/concession €10/free/8; ⊙10am-8pm Tue-Sat; Ⓜ Drassanes or Liceu)

Museu d'Art Contemporani de Barcelona (MACBA)
MUSEUM

2 Map p48, B2

The ever-expanding contemporary art collection of the restlessly dynamic MACBA starts in the Gothic chapel of the Convent dels Àngels and continues in the main gleaming-white building across the square. It's a stage for the best of Catalan, Spanish and international contemporary art. Artists frequently on show include Antoni Tàpies, Miquel Barceló and a host of very-now installation artists. (www.macba.es; Plaça dels Àngels 1; adult/concession €7.50/6; ⊙11am-8pm Mon & Wed-Fri, 10am-8pm Sat, 10am-3pm Sun; Ⓜ Universitat)

Centre de Cultura Contemporània de Barcelona (CCCB)
ARTS CENTRE

3 Map p48, B2

Loved by locals, this dynamic, multi-use cultural centre occupies the shell of an 18th-century hospice. It hosts a constantly changing program of exhibitions on urban design, 20th-century arts, architecture and the city itself. Its photography exhibitions often steal the show, but it's all good. (www.cccb.org; Carrer de Montalegre 5; 2 exhibitions adult/child/concession €7/free/5, free 3-8pm Sun; ⊙11am-8pm Tue-Wed & Fri-Sun, to 10pm Thu; Ⓜ Universitat)

 Top Tip

ArticketBCN

Barcelona's best bargain for art lovers is the **ArticketBCN** (www.articketbcn.org; per person €25), which gives you entry to seven museums for less than half of what you'd pay if you bought individual tickets. The seven museums are MACBA, CCCB, MNAC (p114), Fundació Joan Miró (p118), La Pedrera (p86), Fundació Antoni Tàpies (p94) and the Museu Picasso (p56). The ArticketBCN can be purchased at all participating museums or online at www.barcelonaturisme.com or www.telentrada.com.

Antic Hospital de la Santa Creu

NOTABLE BUILDING

4 Map p48, B3

Gaudí died at this 15th-century hospital, which now houses Catalonia's national library, an arts school and the Institute for Catalan Studies. You can visit the grand reading rooms beneath broad Gothic stone arches, where you'll also find temporary displays of anything from old LPs to medieval monastic hymnals. Its delightful, if somewhat frayed, colonnaded courtyard has a popular cafe. (Carrer de l'Hospital 56; admission free; ◷library 9am-8pm Mon-Fri, to 2pm Sat; Ⓜ Liceu)

Eating

Biblioteca

MEDITERRANEAN €€

5 Map p48, C4

In a long ground-floor setting, with bare brick walls, stylishly simple white decor and an open kitchen, 'The Library' serves up fresh seasonal tastes like *esqueixada* (marinated salt cod served with tomato and peppers) or pigeon with black pudding. It's classy and casual all at once and is a fine example of innovative cooking that never strays too far from its roots. (www.bibliotecarestaurant.cat; Carrer de la Junta de Comerç 28; meals €30-40; ◷8pm-midnight Mon-Sat; Ⓜ Liceu)

Ca L'Estevet

CATALAN €€

6 Map p48, A2

El Raval has numerous restaurants where traditional Catalan cooking still reigns supreme, but this place just shades the others for our money. The lack of a fusty decor helps, as do the carefully prepared daily specials (which sometimes include stuffed meatballs) and menu mainstays such as tender roast kid or homemade Barcelona-style cannelloni. (Carrer de Valldonzella 46; meals €40-50; ◷1.30-4pm Mon, 1.30-4pm & 8-11pm Tue-Sat; Ⓜ Universitat)

Bodega 1800

CATALAN €€

7 Map p48, C3

Owner and chef Ricardo loves nothing better than to come up with a new canapé or delicious snack to offer his tippling guests. He has converted an old wine store into a charming wine bar where you'll linger at the casks or in the adjacent arcade while being guided through snack and wine suggestions. (www.bodega1800.com; Carrer del Carme 31; meals €25-30; ◷noon-4pm & 7-11.30pm Sun-Thu, to midnight Fri & Sat; Ⓜ Liceu)

Museu d'Art Contemporani de Barcelona (p49)

Bar Pinotxo

CATALAN €

 8 Map p48, C3

Of the half-dozen or so tapas bars within the Mercat de la Boqueria, this one near the La Rambla entrance is our favourite, thanks largely to charismatic waiter Juan, who has been here almost four decades. Roll up to the bar and choose the *chucho* (a heavy pastry filled with cream) – irresistible, but not available Mondays – and other fresh market choices. (Mercat de la Boqueria; meals €10-15; ⊘6am-4pm Mon-Sat, closed Aug; MLiceu)

L'Havana

CATALAN €€

9 Map p48, A3

Time stands still in this back-alley, family-run Catalan classic. The front

dining area, with frosted-glass windows, some Modernista design touches and spaciously spread tables, is a touch more severe than the better-lit rear area. Dig into *calamars farcits* (stuffed calamari) and follow it up with some homemade *crema catalana* (a Catalan version of crème brûlée). (Carrer del Lleó 1; meals €25-30; ⊘1-4pm & 8-11.30pm Tue-Sat, 1-4pm Sun; MSant Antoni)

Mesón David

SPANISH €

10 Map p48, B4

With its smoky timber ceiling, excitable staff and chaotic feel, this is a tavern the likes of which are rare these days – a real slice of the old Spain. Plonk yourself down on a bench and enjoy house specialities such as *caldo gallego* (sausage broth). (Carrer de les Carretes 63; meals €15-20; ⊘lunch & dinner Tue-Sun; MParal·lel)

Drinking

Boadas

COCKTAIL BAR

 11 Map p48, C2

One of the city's oldest cocktail bars, Boadas is famed for its daiquiris. The bow-tied waiters have been serving up unique drinkable creations since Miguel Boadas opened the bar in 1933. It specialises in short, intense drinks. The house speciality is the sweetish Boadas, with rum, Dubonnet and Curaçao; Joan Miró and Hemingway tippled here. (Carrer dels Tallers 1; ⊘noon-2am Mon-Thu, to 3am Fri & Sat; MCatalunya)

Casa Almirall

BAR

12 Map p48, A3

People have been boozing here since 1860, making it the oldest continuously functioning bar in the city. Delightfully dishevelled, dark and intriguing, it still has its original Modernista bar and a cast-iron statue of the muse of the 1888 World Fair. (Carrer de Joaquín Costa 33; 🕑5.30pm-2.30am Sun-Thu, 7pm-3am Fri & Sat; MUniversitat)

London Bar

BAR

13 Map p48, C4

In the heart of the once-notorious Barri Xinès district, this bar was founded in 1910 as a hang-out for circus hands, and drew the likes of Picasso and Miró in search of local colour. With the occasional band playing out the back and a wonderful mix of local customers and travellers, it remains a classic. (Carrer Nou de la Rambla 34; 🕑7.30pm-4am Tue-Sun; MDrassanes)

Local Life

Barrio Bar

Bar Pastis (Map p48, D4; www.barpastis.com; Carrer de Santa Mònica 4; 🕑7.30pm-2am Sun-Fri, to 3am Sat; MDrassanes) has seen it all and weathered El Raval's changes with the dispassionate air of an old-timer who ain't goin' nowhere. French cabaret *chanson*, bossa nova and tango all get a run in this pleasingly cluttered shoebox of a bar, which has been in business since WWII.

Marmalade

BAR

14 Map p48, B3

From the street you can see the golden hues of the backlit bar way down the end of a long, lounge-lined passageway. To the left of the bar, by a bare brick wall, is a pool table – popular but somehow out of place in this chic, ill-lit chill den. Some of the cocktails here go for just €5 and none cost more than €7. (www.marmaladebarcelona.com; Carrer de la Riera Alta 4-6; 🕑7pm-3am; MSant Antoni)

Moog

CLUB

15 Map p48, D4

Moog (named after the synthesiser) is reliable for techno and electronica, and is always packed with a young, enthusiastic crowd. Bigger in stature than in size, it attracts lots of big-name DJs. Upstairs it specialises in indie retro pop numbers and is better for conversation. (www.masimas.com/moog; Carrer de l'Arc del Teatre 3; admission €10; 🕑midnight-5am; MDrassanes)

Bar Muy Buenas

BAR

16 Map p48, B3

What started life as a late-19th-century milk bar is now lacking the milk, but the Modernista decor and relaxed company make this a great bar for a quiet *mojito*, some live music and Middle Eastern nibbles. (Carrer del Carme 63; 🕑9am-2am Mon-Thu, 10am-3am Fri & Sat, 7pm-2am Sun; MLiceu)

Betty Ford BAR

17 Map p48, A2

This enticing corner bar is a good stop along the student-jammed run of Carrer de Joaquín Costa. It does nice cocktails and fills with an even mix of 30-something locals and foreigners, and an abundance of tattoos and piercings. (Carrer de Joaquín Costa 56; ⏱6pm-1.30am Mon, 2pm-1.30am Tue-Thu, 2pm-2.30am Fri & Sat; Ⓜ Universitat)

Bodega La Penúltima BAR

18 Map p48, A3

There is a baroque semidarkness about this dark-timber and sunset-yellow place. In Spanish lore, one never drinks *la última* (the last one); it's bad luck. So here, a mixed group huddles at the bar or crowds into lumpy lounges for endless 'second-last rounds' of wine, beer or cocktails. (Carrer de la Riera Alta 40; ⏱7pm-2am Tue-Thu, to 3am Fri & Sat, to 1am Sun; Ⓜ Sant Antoni)

Shopping

Castelló MUSIC

19 Map p48, B2

This family-run music store has been tickling the ears of Catalans since 1935, although its five stores have recently shrunk to one. It has a huge range of CDs across all genres, including classical, with a carefully chosen catalogue of vinyl out the back. The location is perfect as the street is home to plenty of other music-oriented shops. (www.

castellodiscos.com; Carrer dels Tallers 7; ⏱10am-8.30pm Mon-Sat; Ⓜ Catalunya)

La Portorriqueña FOOD & DRINK

20 Map p48, B2

Forget Starbucks; this is coffee. Beans from around the world are freshly ground before your eyes in the combination of your choice and the smell is simply wonderful. This place has been in the coffee business since 1902 but also purveys all sorts of chocolate goodies. (Carrer d'en Xuclà 25; ⏱9am-2pm & 5-8pm Mon-Fri, 9am-2pm Sat; Ⓜ Catalunya)

El Indio HOMEWARES

21 Map p48, C3

You may not want to buy anything at 'The Indian', but just walking into this fabric store with the Modernista shopfront is like stepping a century back in time. The service is old-style, and you'll find everything from sheets and tablecloths to FC Barcelona towels. (Carrer del Carme 24; ⏱10am-2pm & 4-8pm Mon-Sat; Ⓜ Liceu)

Against HOMEWARES

22 Map p48, B2

Lovers of retro will adore this treasure trove of furnishings and decorative items in the heart of El Raval. Most of the offerings date from the 1960s or '50s – mid-century furniture is the motto. It's mostly designer stuff (think Frank Lloyd Wright and his ilk) and mostly from Spain, France and Italy. (www.againstbcn.com; Carrer del Notariet 9; ⏱4-8.30pm Mon-Fri, 11am-2pm Sat; Ⓜ Liceu)

Explore

La Ribera
& Parc de la Ciutadella

In La Ribera is one of Barcelona's most beguiling corners: El Born. The old town's epicentre in medieval times, leafy Passeig del Born is again abuzz, crammed with bars, restaurants and boutiques. Adding to the neighbourhood's appeal, La Ribera also boasts the Museu Picasso, Barcelona's mightiest Gothic church, a wonderful market and the largest park in downtown Barcelona.

The Sights in a Day

☼ In a bid to avoid the crowds, get to the **Museu Picasso** (p56) early, then take a guided tour of the **Palau de la Música Catalana** (p64) to fully appreciate the genius and eccentricity of Modernisme. The **Mercat de Santa Caterina** (p64) is perfect for stocking up for a picnic lunch in the **Parc de la Ciutadella** (p64).

☼ Explore the park after lunch, then head to the **Museu de la Xocolata** (p65) for dessert. After such sinful pleasures, settle into a pew to admire the grace and splendour of the **Església de Santa Maria del Mar** (p58). The church is just as beautiful on the outside so make for our favourite vantage point, **La Vinya del Senyor** (p68), until evening falls.

☾ The choice of tapas in El Born is endless, but we'd start with *cava* (sparkling wine) and anchovies at **El Xampanyet** (p61), follow it with something offbeat at **Bar del Pla** (p61), then fight for a bar stool at **Cal Pep** (p61). After dinner, enjoy a *mojito* at **Cactus Bar** (p61), next to Passeig del Born.

For a local's night out in El Born, see p60.

◉ Top Sights

Museu Picasso (p56)

Església de Santa Maria del Mar (p58)

◯ Local Life

Tapas & Bar Hopping in El Born (p60)

♥ Best of Barcelona

Tapas

El Xampanyet (p61)

Comerç 24 (p67)

Cal Pep (p61)

Bubó (p61)

Centre Cultural Euskal Etxea (p61)

Wine & Cocktail Bars

La Vinya del Senyor (p68)

Cactus Bar (p61)

Shopping

Custo Barcelona (p71)

Olisoliva (p70)

Getting There

Ⓜ **Metro** Jaume I station (line 4), on the southwestern side of La Ribera, is close to everything.

Ⓜ **Metro** Urquinaona (lines 1 and 4) is handy for the Palau de la Música Catalana, while Arc de Triomf (line 1) is good for Parc de la Ciutadella.

Top Sights
Museu Picasso

Pablo Picasso spent many years in Barcelona and, suitably, the city hosts the world's foremost museum dedicated to the artist's formative years and his extraordinary early talent; the cubist paintings for which he is best known are largely absent, but this is nonetheless a world-class gallery that traces his development as an artist. The building – five contiguous medieval stone mansions that span five centuries and yet have seamlessly become one – is itself a perfectly conceived work of art.

⊙ Map p62, D3

www.museupicasso.bcn.cat

Carrer de Montcada 15-23

adult/child/concession €10/free/6, free Sun 3-8pm, audio guide €3

⊙10am-8pm Tue-Sun

Ⓜ Jaume I

Works from Picasso's 1957 *Las Meninas (Infanta Margarita María)* series on display in Museu Picasso

Don't Miss

The Early Years
ROOMS 3 & 5

Picasso's early endeavours show a precocious talent searching for his style. In Room 3, his *Science & Charity* (painted at age 16 in 1897) is proof that, had he wanted, Picasso would have made a fine conventional artist. In Room 5, his studies of the styles of Velázquez and El Greco are fascinating insights into an artist perfecting his craft.

The Blue Period
ROOM 8

Before cubism took him across unexplored creative frontiers, Picasso went through his first thematic adventure – the Blue Period. Lasting from 1901 to 1904, it coincided with his last years spent living in Barcelona. His nocturnal blue-tinted views of *Terrats de Barcelona* (Rooftops of Barcelona) and *El Foll* (The Madman) are cold and cheerless, and yet somehow spectrally alive.

Early Cubism
ROOM 11

Picasso's masterworks lie elsewhere, but by 1917 his style was hinting at the cubist forms to come. During a six-month stay in Barcelona in 1917, he painted *Passeig de Colom* and *Blanquita Suárez,* which bear strong evidence of what was to follow.

The Velázquez Obsession
ROOMS 12–14

The extent to which Picasso was influenced by the great masters is evident in these rooms, which contain an extraordinary 58-painting study of Diego Velázquez' masterpiece *Las Meninas* (which hangs in the Museo del Prado in Madrid). Painted in Cannes in 1957, these will satisfy your longing for Picasso's signature cubist style.

☑ Top Tips

▸ Understand this gallery for what it is: a fascinating insight into Picasso's early work with scarcely a cubist masterpiece in sight.

▸ This is one of Barcelona's most popular museums – get here early and be prepared to wait.

▸ Consider buying ArticketBCN (see the boxed text, p49) for combined admission to this and six other museums for €25.

✗ Take a Break

On Picasso's last visit to the city in 1934, El Xampanyet (p61) had already been open five years; it's still great for tapas.

Traditional Spanish tapas with subtle creative twists are the order of the day at young-at-heart Bar del Pla (p61), a little further northwest along Carrer de Montcada.

Top Sights
Església de Santa Maria del Mar

Nothing prepares you for the singular beauty of Església de Santa Maria del Mar. Barcelona's most stirring Gothic structure, the church stands serenely amid the crowds and clutter of buildings in El Born. In contrast to the tight warren of neighbouring streets, a real sense of light and space pervades the entire sanctuary of the church. Its interior is close to perfection wrought in stone, making this a worthy rival to La Catedral and La Sagrada Família for the affections of visitors to the city.

Map p62, D4

Plaça de Santa Maria del Mar

admission free

9am-1.30pm & 5.30-8.30pm

M Jaume I

The soaring interior of Església de Santa Maria del Mar

Don't Miss

Main Sanctuary

The pleasing unity of form and symmetry of the church's central nave and two flanking aisles owes much to the rapidity with which it was built in the 14th century – a mere 59 years, which must be a record for a major European house of worship. The slender, octagonal pillars create an enormous sense of lateral space bathed in the light of stained glass.

Ceiling & Side Chapels

Even before anarchists gutted the church in 1909 and again in 1936, Santa Maria always lacked superfluous decoration. Gone are the gilded chapels that weigh heavily over many Spanish churches, while the splashes of colour high above the nave are subtle – unusually and beautifully so. It all serves to highlight the church's fine proportions, purity of line and sense of space.

The Porters

Look closely at the stones throughout the main sanctuary. One day a week during construction, the city's *bastaixos* (porters) carried these stones on their backs from the royal quarry in Montjuïc to the construction site. The memory of them lives on in reliefs in the main doors and stone carvings in the church, a reminder that this was conceived as a people's church.

El Fossar de les Moreres

Opposite the church's southern flank, an eternal flame burns high over a sunken square. This was El Fossar de les Moreres (the Mulberry Cemetery), where Catalan resistance fighters were buried after the siege of Barcelona ended in defeat in September 1714 during the War of the Spanish Succession.

☑ Top Tips

▶ If your purpose is spiritual, try to be here for the daily mass at 7.30pm.

▶ Prayers are held in numerous languages, followed by a brief organ recital at noon on Thursdays, from May to September.

▶ Ask in the gift shop in case evening baroque music recitals are scheduled.

✕ Take a Break

Sit out the lunchtime hours when the church is closed at one of the outdoor tables at Bubó (p61), where tapas is accompanied by fine views of the western facade.

While you're waiting for the church to reopen, head upstairs for one of two balcony tables and choose from around 350 wines at La Vinya del Senyor (p68).

Local Life
Tapas & Bar Hopping in El Born

If there's one place that distils Barcelona's enduring cool to its essence and provides a snapshot of all that's irresistible about this city, it has to be El Born, the tangle of streets surrounding the Església de Santa Maria del Mar. Its secret is simple: this is where locals go for an authentic Barcelona night out.

1 Passeig del Born
Most nights, and indeed most things, in El Born begin along the Passeig del Born, one of the prettiest little boulevards in Europe. It's a place to sit as much as to promenade. It's a graceful setting beneath the trees from which El Born's essential appeal is obvious – thronging people, brilliant bars and architecture that springs from a medieval film set.

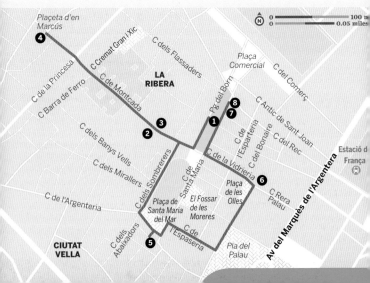

❷ Catalan Tapas

Push through the crowd, order a *cava* (sparkling wine) and an assortment of tapas at **El Xampanyet** (Carrer de Montcada 22; ⏱lunch & dinner Tue-Sat, lunch Sun; Ⓜ Jaume I), one of the city's best-known *cava* bars, in business since 1929. Star dishes include tangy *boquerons en vinagre* (white anchovies in vinegar) and there's high-quality seafood served from a can in the Catalan way.

❸ Best of Basque

Having taken your first lesson in Barcelona-style tapas it's time to compare it with the *pintxos* (Basque tapas of food morsels perched atop pieces of bread) lined up along the bar at **Centre Cultural Euskal Etxea** (Placeta de Montcada 1; ⏱lunch & dinner Tue-Sat, lunch Sun; Ⓜ Jaume I), a real slice of San Sebastián.

❹ Spain with a Twist

This detour to the northern limits of El Born is worth the walk. At first glance, the tapas at informal **Bar del Pla** (www.elpla.cat; Carrer de Montcada 2; ⏱noon-11.30pm; Ⓜ Jaume I) are traditionally Spanish, but the riffs on a theme show an assured touch. Try the ham and roasted-meat croquettes or the marinated salmon, yoghurt and mustard.

❺ Tapas with a View

Back in the heart of El Born, in the shadow of Església de Santa Maria del Mar, pastry chef Carles Mampel operates **Bubó** (www.bubo.ws; Carrer de les Caputxes 6 & 10; ⏱9am-1am Sun-Thu, to 2am Fri & Sat; Ⓜ Jaume I). If you're not already sated, try the salted cod croquettes at one of the outdoor tables inching onto the lovely square.

❻ Cal Pep

Boisterous **Cal Pep** (www.calpep.com; Plaça de les Olles 8; ⏱dinner Mon, lunch & dinner Tue-Fri, lunch Sat, closed Aug; Ⓜ Barceloneta) is one of Barcelona's enduring stars. It can be difficult to snaffle a bar stool from which to order gourmet bar snacks such as *cloïsses amb pernil* (clams with ham); if they're all full, order a drink and wait. It's always worth it.

❼ El Born's Favourite Bar

El Born Bar (Passeig del Born 26; ⏱5.30pm-2am; Ⓜ Jaume I) effortlessly attracts everyone from cool 30-somethings from all over town to locals who pass judgment on Passeig del Born's passing parade. Its staying power depends on a good selection of beers and spirits and (if you're still hungry) decent tinned tapas.

❽ The Last Mojito

So many Barcelona nights end with a *mojito*, and El Born's biggest and best are to be found at **Cactus Bar** (www.cactusbar.cat; Passeig del Born 30; ⏱10am-4am; Ⓜ Jaume I). The outdoor tables next to Passeig del Born are the perfect way to wind down the night.

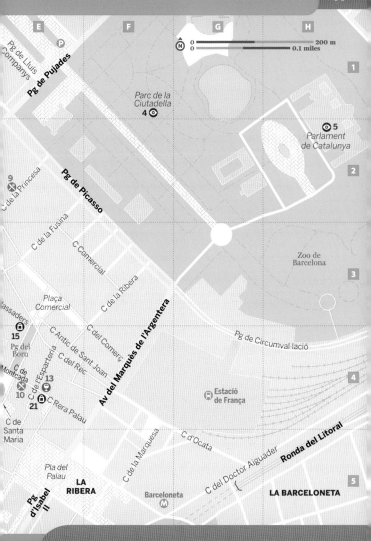

E
F
G
H

Pg de Lluís
Companys

Pg de Pujades

Parc de la
Ciutadella
4 ⊙

⊙5
*Parlament
de Catalunya*

1

2

C de la Princesa
9

Pg de Picasso

C de la Fusina

C Comercial

C de la Ribera

Zoo de
Barcelona

3

assaders

Plaça
Comercial

C Antic de Sant Joan

C del Comerç

Av del Marquès de l'Argentera

Pg de Circumval·lació

15
Pg del
Born

C de l'Esparteria

C del Rec

C de
Montcada

13

10

21

C Rera Palau

Estació
de França

4

C de
Santa
Maria

Pla del
Palau

C de la Marquesa

C d'Ocata

C del Doctor Aiguader

Ronda del Litoral

Pg
d'Isabel II

**LA
RIBERA**

Barceloneta
Ⓜ

C del Doctor Aiguader

LA BARCELONETA

5

0 ———— 200 m
0 ———— 0.1 miles

Sights

Palau de la Música Catalana
NOTABLE BUILDING

1 Map p62, A2

The Palace of Catalan Music drips with all the fevered imagination that Modernista architect Lluís Domènech i Montaner could muster. Finished in 1908, this World Heritage gem remains an enchanting concert setting. The exterior and foyer are opulent, but these are nothing compared with the interior of the main auditorium. Fifty-minute tours run every half-hour. (www.palaumusica.org; Carrer del Palau de la Música 4-6; tours adult/child/concession €12/free/10; ⏱10am-6pm Aug, 10am-3.30pm Sep-Jul; ⓂUrquinaona)

Mercat de Santa Caterina
MARKET

2 Map p62, C3

Though it lacks the clamour of the Mercat de la Boqueria, this 21st-century produce market with its undulating, polychrome-tiled roof is an atmospheric place to stop for lunch or shop for fresh produce and gourmet products. Local architect Enric Miralles designed it on the site of its 19th-century predecessor, which itself replaced a medieval Dominican monastery. (www.mercatsantacaterina.net; Avinguda de Francesc Cambó 16; ⏱7.30am-2pm Mon, to 3.30pm Tue, Wed & Sat, to 8.30pm Thu & Fri; ⓂJaume I)

Museu Barbier-Mueller d'Art Pre-Colombí
MUSEUM

3 Map p62, D4

In this small but outstanding museum you'll find a sparkling assortment of art from the pre-Columbian civilisations of Central and South America. Gold glitters in the form of highly intricate ornamental objects, expressive masks and women's jewellery. These pieces are complemented by statuary, ceramics, textiles, and ritual and household objects from all over South America. (www.barbier-mueller. ch; Carrer de Montcada 12-14; adult/child/concession €3.50/free/1.70, free 1st Sun of month; ⏱11am-7pm Tue-Fri, to 8pm Sat & Sun; ⓂJaume I)

Parc de la Ciutadella
PARK

4 Map p62, F1

The verdant Parc de la Ciutadella is the site of Catalonia's regional parliament, the city zoo, some eye-catching buildings and the monumental *Cascada* (waterfall) created between 1875 and 1881 by Josep Fontsère with the help of a young Antoni Gaudí. The park was created when the hated 18th-century Ciutadella fortress, built by Madrid to keep watch over the restless population, was demolished. (Passeig de Picasso; ⏱8am-9pm; ⓂArc de Triomf or Barceloneta)

Glass ceiling of the Palau de la Música Catalana

Parlament de Catalunya
NOTABLE BUILDING

5 Map p62, H2

In the middle of Parc de la Ciutadella, in what used to be the fortress's former arsenal, now sits Catalonia's parliament, a powerful symbol of Catalan identity. On weekends, visitors can head up the sweeping Escala d'Honor (Stairway of Honour) and through several solemn halls to see the Saló de Sessions, the semicircular auditorium where parliament sits. (☏93 304 66 45; www.parlament.cat; Parc de la Ciutadella; admission free; ⊙10am-7pm Sat, to 2pm Sun; Ⓜ Barceloneta or Arc de Triomf)

Museu de la Xocolata
MUSEUM

6 Map p62, D2

Explore the sticky story of chocolate through audiovisual displays (in English on request), touch-screen presentations, historical exhibits and the somewhat kitsch chocolate models of anything from La Sagrada Família to Winnie the Pooh. (www.pastisseria.com; Plaça de Pons i Clerch; adult/child/concession €4.30/free/3.65, 1st Mon of month free; ⊙10am-7pm Mon-Sat, to 3pm Sun; Ⓜ Jaume I)

Museu Europeu d'Art Modern (MEAM)
MUSEUM

7 Map p62, D3

Barcelona's newest museum, the European Museum of Modern Art opened in the summer of 2011 in the Palau

Understand

Catalan Gothic

- -

The Historical Context

The emergence of the soaring Gothic style of architecture in France in
the 13th century coincided with an expanding Catalan empire, the rise
of a trading class and a burgeoning mercantile sphere of influence. The
enormous cost of building the grand new monuments could thus be
covered by the steady increase in Barcelona's wealth.

The architectural style reflected developing building techniques. The
introduction of flying buttresses and ribbed vaulting in ceilings allowed
engineers to raise edifices loftier and seemingly lighter than ever before.
The pointed arch became standard and great rose windows offered a
way to light inside these enormous spaces.

Catalan Difference

Catalan Gothic rarely followed the same course as the style in northern
Europe. Decorations are more sparing and another distinctive characteristic is the triumph of breadth over height. While northern European
cathedrals reach for the sky, Catalan Gothic structures push to the
sides, stretching the vaulting design to the limit.

The Saló del Tinell in the Museu d'Història de Barcelona (p34), with
a parade of 15m arches (among the largest ever built without reinforce-
ment) holding up the roof, is a perfect example of Catalan Gothic.
Another is the present home of the Museu Marítim (p79), Barcelona's
medieval shipyards. In churches too, the Catalans opted for robust
shape and lateral space – step into the Església de Santa Maria del Mar
(p58) and you'll soon get the idea.

Also a notable departure from northern Gothic styles is the lack of
spires and pinnacles. Bell towers tend to terminate in a flat or nearly flat
roof. Occasional exceptions prove the rule. The main facade of Barcelona's Catedral, with its three gnarled and knobbly spires, does vaguely
resemble the outline that confronts you in the cathedrals of Chartres or
Cologne. But then this was a 19th-century addition, admittedly constructed to an existing medieval design.

Most of Barcelona's Gothic heritage lies within the boundaries of the
old city but a few examples can be found beyond, notably the Museu-
Monestir de Pedralbes (p133) in Sarrià.

Gomis, a handsome 18th-century mansion around the corner from the Museu Picasso. It has an exciting collection that focuses on contemporary figurative art from across Europe. (www.meam.es, in Catalan & Spanish; Carrer de Barra de Ferro 5; adult/child/concession €7/free/5; ⏱10am-8pm Tue-Sun; Ⓜ Jaume I)

Eating

Comerç 24

FUSION €€€

8 ⊗ Map p62, D1

In the vanguard of Barcelona's modern eateries, this Michelin-starred place is a witches' den of almost infernal variety and extremes. The decor is predominantly black and yellow, the cuisine eclectic and the owner-chef, Carles Abellán, an alumnus of masterchef Ferran Adrià and award-winning restaurant elBulli. The emphasis is on waves of bite-sized snacks that traverse the culinary globe, with foams and curious combinations of taste. (📞93 319 21 02; www.comerc24.com; Carrer del Comerç 24; set menus €75-100; ⏱lunch & dinner Tue-Sat; Ⓜ Arc de Triomf)

Espai Sucre

FUSION €€

9 ⊗ Map p62, E2

This extraordinary place claims to have been the first dessert restaurant in the world. Although its flavours now span sweet and savoury, the philosophy remains unchanged, with offerings such as goat cheesecake with raspberries, red pepper and ginger, or cod rice with tomato ice cream, arti-

chokes and honey. Choose from one of the set menus and enjoy a unique dining experience. (📞93 268 16 30; www.espaisucre.com; Carrer de la Princesa 53; meals €35-55; ⏱dinner Tue-Sat; Ⓜ Jaume I)

La Llavor dels Orígens

CATALAN €€

10 ⊗ Map p62, E4

A treasure chest of Catalan regional products, this place offers nicely presented bite-sized dishes (mostly €5 to €8), including duck with pear, or squid, *butifarra* (Catalan sausage), mushrooms and peas, all mixed and matched with Catalan wine by the glass. The decor is intimate and you'll eat surrounded by wine bottles. The tapas menu (€19.20) is a steal. (www.lallavordelsorigens. com; Carrer de la Vidrieria 6-8; meals €20-25; ⏱12.30pm-12.30am; Ⓜ Jaume I; 🥗)

Local Life

Fish for People in the Know

There's no sign, but locals know where to head for a feast. The raw ingredients at **El Passadís del Pep** (Map p62, E5; www.passadis.com; Pla del Palau 2; meals €50-60; ⏱ dinner Mon, lunch & dinner Tue-Sat Sep-Jul; Ⓜ Barceloneta) are delivered from fishing ports along the Catalan coast. There's no menu – what's on offer depends on what the sea has surrendered that day. Just head down the ill-lit corridor and entrust yourself to the restaurant's care.

Pla de la Garsa
CATALAN €€

11 🍴 Map p62, D3

This 17th-century house is ideal for a romantic dinner. Timber beams, anarchically scattered tables and soft ambient music combine to make an enchanting setting over two floors for traditional Catalan cooking, such as black pudding with mushrooms. Other specialities include salted cod or marinated sardines, and the sturgeon carpaccio with champagne vinaigrette is filled with flavour. (Carrer dels Assaonadors 13; meals €25-30; ⊙dinner; Ⓜ Jaume I)

Cuines de Santa Caterina
MEDITERRANEAN €€

With a contemporary feel, open kitchens and decor as fresh as the food it serves, this multifaceted eatery inside the Mercat de Santa Caterina (see **2** ◎ Map p62, C3) does everything from breakfast through to evening tapas. Peck at the sushi bar, tuck into classic rice dishes or go vegetarian. Service can be brisk and it's first come, first served for tables. (www.cuinessantacaterina.com, in Spanish; Mercat de Santa Caterina; meals €25-30 ⊙9am-11.30pm Sun-Wed, to 12.30am Thu-Sat; Ⓜ Jaume I)

Drinking

La Vinya del Senyor
WINE BAR

12 🍷 Map p62, D5

A wine-taster's fantasy, this bar's glorious location looks out over the Església de Santa Maria del Mar. You

Fusion cuisine at Comerç 24 (p67)

can choose from around 350 varieties of wine and *cava* from around the world (by the bottle or half or full glass to suit all budgets) and enjoy inventive *platillos* (mini-tapas) as you sip your drink. Try to grab the table by the window upstairs. (Plaça de Santa Maria del Mar 5; ⊙noon-1am Mon-Thu, to 2am Fri & Sat, to midnight Sun; Ⓜ Jaume I)

Mudanzas
BAR

13 🍷 Map p62, E4

This was one of the first bars to get things into gear in El Born and its winning formula of marble-topped tables and chequered floors still attracts a faithful crowd. It's a straightforward place for a beer, a chat and a few tapas. Oh, and it does a nice line in Italian *grappa*. There are also extensive choices in whisky and other spirits. (Carrer de la Vidrieria 15; ⏱10am-2.30am; Ⓜ Jaume I)

Entertainment

Palau de la Música Catalana
LIVE MUSIC

Aside from being a beacon of Modernisme, the multi-use Palau de la Música Catalana (see 1 ◎ Map p62; A2) hosts an eclectic musical program, including flamenco, classical and choral, in both the stunning main theatre and the smaller, modern chamber-orchestra auditorium. It has an excellent cafe, too. (☏902 442882; www.palaumusica. org; Carrer del Palau de la Música; tickets €10-150; ⏱box office 10am-9pm Mon-Sat; Ⓜ Urquinaona)

Ｑ Local Life

A Fine Cut

You know a place must be good when, in streets thronging with tourists, the customers are all local. One such place is **La Botifarreria** (Map p62; D4; www.labotifarreria.com, in Catalan & Spanish; Carrer de Santa Maria 4; ⏱8.30am-2.30pm & 5-8pm Mon-Fri, 8.30am-2.30pm Sat; Ⓜ Jaume I), which sells cheeses, hams and snacks. The mainstay here is an astounding variety of handcrafted sausages. Many are fresh and ready for cooking, but there are just as many you'll want to buy for your picnic or for a gift back home.

Shopping

Casa Gispert
FOOD & DRINK

14 🔒 Map p62, D4

Nuts and coffee are roasted in a wood-fired oven at this wonderfully aromatic wholesaler that's been perfecting its technique since 1851. Hazelnuts and almonds are the specialities, complemented by piles of dried fruit and a host of artisanal products, such as mustards and preserves. (www. casagispert.com; Carrer dels Sombrerers 23; ⏱9am-2pm & 4-8.30pm Tue-Sat; Ⓜ Jaume I)

Hofmann Patisseria
FOOD & DRINK

15 🔒 Map p62, E4

With old timber cabinets, this gourmet patisserie has an air of timelessness, although everything is baked by recent graduates of one of Barcelona's more prestigious cooking schools. Choose between jars of delicious chocolates, pastries or an array of cakes and other sweets. Hofmann recently won the much-coveted prize for the best butter croissant in Spain. (www. hofmann-bcn.com; Carrer dels Flassaders 44; ⏱9am-2pm & 3.30-8pm Mon-Thu, to 8.30pm Fri & Sat, 9am-2.30pm Sun; Ⓜ Jaume I)

Arlequí Màscares
ARTS & CRAFTS

16 🔒 Map p62, C4

A wonderful little oasis of originality, this shop specialises in masks for costume and decoration. Some of the pieces are superb, while stock also includes a beautiful range of decorative

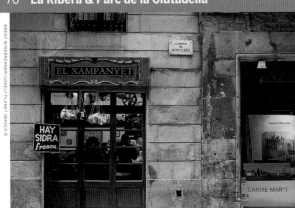

El Xampanyet (p61) tapas bar in La Ribera

boxes in Catalan themes. (www.arlequi
mask.com; Carrer de la Princesa 7; ⊙10.30am-
8.30pm Mon-Sat, 11am-7pm Sun; M Jaume I)

Olisoliva
FOOD & DRINK

Inside the Mercat de Santa Caterina
(see 2 ⊙ Map p62, C3), this store is
stacked with olive oils and vinegars
from all over Spain. Taste some of the
products with bread before decid-
ing. Some of the world's best olive
oils come from southern Spain, and
the owners will be happy to explain
the wonders of any number of their
products. (www.olisoliva.com, in Spanish;
Mercat de Santa Caterina; ⊙9am-2pm Mon,
9am-3.30pm Tue, Wed & Sat, 9am-3.30pm &
5-8.30pm Thu & Fri; M Jaume I)

Taller Antic
ANTIQUES

17 🔒 Map p62, C4

Step back in time as you handle the
delicate silver and glassware in this
shop. Old-style perfume bottles and
the kind of accessories ladies and
gents might have used in the 19th
century make this a nostalgic's corner
of paradise. (Carrer de la Princesa 14;
⊙10.30am-3pm & 4.30-8pm Mon & Tue,
10.30am-8pm Wed-Sat, 10.30am-5.30pm Sun;
M Jaume I)

El Magnífico
FOOD & DRINK

18 🔒 Map p62, D4

Take a veritable tour of world coffee
with the friendly Sans family. They
had so much fun with their beans and

blends that they opened another store across the street. (www.cafesel magnifico.com, in Catalan & Spanish; Carrer de l'Argenteria 64; ⏱10am-2pm & 4-8pm Mon-Fri, 10am-2pm & 4.30-8pm Sat; Ⓜ Jaume I)

Sans & Sans
FOOD & DRINK

19 🔒 Map p62, D4

Run by the Sans family of El Magnífico fame, Sans & Sans is devoted to more than 200 types of tea. (www. sansisans-finetea.com; Carrer de l'Argenteria 59; ⏱10am-2pm & 4-8pm Mon-Fri, 10am-2pm & 4.30-8pm Sat; Ⓜ Jaume I)

Vila Viniteca
FOOD & DRINK

20 🔒 Map p62, D5

This unassuming shop has a superb range of Spanish and international wines, from cheap table varieties to vintage treasures, sold by enthusiastic staff. This place knows its stuff, having been in the business since 1932. At No 9 the same owners have another store devoted to gourmet food products, with a restaurant downstairs. (www.vila viniteca.es, in Spanish; Carrer dels Agullers 7 & 9; ⏱8.30am-8.30pm Mon-Sat; Ⓜ Jaume I)

Custo Barcelona
FASHION

21 🔒 Map p62, E4

Created in the early 1980s by the Dalmau brothers, Custo is the biggest name in contemporary Barcelona fashion and one of its trendiest exports. The dazzling colours and cuts of anything from dinner jackets to hot pants are for the uninhibited. It has five other outlets around town. (www. custo-barcelona.com; Plaça de les Olles 7; ⏱10am-10pm Mon-Sat; Ⓜ Barceloneta)

Explore

Barceloneta & the Beaches

Barcelona's waterfront is a fascinating corner of the city – a place where avant-garde public art is juxtaposed with the gritty thorough-fares of La Barceloneta, an 18th-century fisherfolk's district. It's in the restaurants of the latter that you'll find the city's best seafood and rice dishes, while beaches stretch away to the north.

The Sights in a Day

☀ La Barceloneta has few stand-out sights and they're easily ticked off in a morning. Begin with a journey through Catalan history at the **Museu d'Història de Catalunya** (p78), take a return trip aboard the **Transbordador Aeri** (p78) for fine waterfront views, then head for **L'Aquàrium** (p78), one of Spain's best aquariums.

☀ Most afternoons in La Barceloneta revolve around food and beaches. For the former, we suggest tapas at **El Vaso de Oro** (p75) or **Can Paixano** (p74), but leave room for a sit-down meal at **Suquet de l'Almirall** (p79). The perfect response to such gastronomic excess is to lie down, and this is best done at any beach that takes your fancy from La Barceloneta to Port Olímpic and beyond.

☾ You're unlikely to want to stray too far from the water's edge even after the sun sets. But for a different vibe to La Barceloneta, follow the shoreline north to Port Olímpic for a drink. It's the scene for all kinds of agreeably chilled waterfront places. If you're up for another meal, try **Xiringuito d'Escribà** (p81).

For a local's day by the beach, see p74.

 Local Life

Sea & Seafood (p74)

 Best of Barcelona

Seafood Restaurants
Suquet de l'Almirall (p79)

Can Solé (p81)

Cheriff (p81)

Torre d'Alta Mar (p82)

Getting There

Ⓜ **Metro** Drassanes (line 3) is best for the southwestern end of the port, Barceloneta (line 4) for La Barceloneta, and Ciutadella Vila Olímpica (line 4) for the beaches and Port Olímpic.

🚌 **Bus** Numbers 17, 39 and 64 all converge on La Barceloneta.

🚠 **Cable Car** If you're coming from Montjuïc, the Transbordador Aeri (cable car) is best.

Local Life
Sea & Seafood

Barcelona's Mediterranean roots are nowhere more pronounced than in La Barceloneta, a seaside peninsula with a salty air and an enduring relationship with the sea. As often as not, this is one area where locals outnumber tourists, at least on weekends when the city's restaurants and beaches throng with a predominantly local crowd.

❶ The First Tipple

Welcome to Barcelona as it once was. It doesn't come any more authentic than **Can Paixano** (Carrer de la Reina Cristina 7; ⏰9am-10.30pm; Ⓜ Barceloneta), one of the best old-style *cava* (sparkling wine) bars in Barcelona. Tucked away amid cheap electronics stores, this ageless bar serves up the pink stuff in elegant little glasses, provided you can elbow your way through the crowds to order.

❷ Beer & Prawns

If you like noisy, crowded bars, high-speed staff ready with a smile and a wisecrack, a cornucopia of tapas and the illusion, in here at least, that Barcelona hasn't changed in decades, come to **El Vaso de Oro** (Carrer de Balboa 6; ⏰11am-midnight; Ⓜ Barceloneta). This place brews its own beers and the tapas are delicious (try the grilled prawns).

❸ The Real Deal

Refugees from fashionable food in search of a hearty feed and a bottle of cold *turbio* (a cloudy and pleasing white wine) huddle on the communal benches at **Can Maño** (Carrer del Baluard 12; ⏰lunch & dinner Mon-Sat; Ⓜ Barceloneta) and get stuck into *raciones* (plate-sized serves) of all sorts of seafood. A long-lived, no-nonsense family business, it generally attracts queues.

❹ A Waterfront Stroll

Maybe it's a good thing the Metro doesn't reach the beach at La Barceloneta, obliging you to walk down the sunny portside promenade of **Passeig de Joan de Borbó**. Megayachts sway gently on your right as you bowl down a street crackling with activity and drawing a cross-section of Barcelona society.

❺ The Last Fisherfolk

In these days of commercial fishing fleets, it's reassuring to find a city of Barcelona's size and prestige still carrying out fishing in the old way.

Barcelona's small fleet, which supplies many of La Barceloneta's restaurants, ties up along the **Moll del Rellotge**.

❻ Designer Ice Cream

You might think that you're full, but it's worth visiting **Vioko** (Passeig Joan de Borbó 55; ⏰1pm-midnight; Ⓜ Barceloneta) just to try the extraordinary taste sensation that comes from flavouring ice cream with Catalonia's favourite dessert, *crema catalana* (a rich custard). If you need a second flavour to make up the cone, make it vanilla. Bliss.

❼ Barcelona's Beaches

A day at the beach is a long-standing Barcelona tradition, and even those who can't escape the city in summer will spend their afternoons here. There are prettier beaches elsewhere on earth, but none so handy for the world's coolest city. **Platja de Sant Sebastià**, closest to Barceloneta, yields to **Platja de la Barceloneta**, and both are broad and agreeably long sweeps of sand.

❽ An Olympic Port

A 1.25km promenade shadows the waterfront all the way to the crammed marina of **Port Olímpic** (Ⓜ Ciutadella Vila Olímpica), which was created for the 1992 Olympics and is still the glamorous end of Barcelona's waterfront. An eye-catcher on the approach from La Barceloneta is Frank Gehry's giant copper *Peix* (Fish) sculpture, while just to the north is the agreeable **Platja de Nova Icària**.

E
C de Wellington
Universitat Pompeu Fabra
Parc de Carles I
Ⓜ Ciutadella Vila Olímpica

F
C de Moscou
C de Salvador Espriu
Plaça dels Voluntaris
C de Ramon Trias Fargas
C de la Marina

Av del Litoral

G
11 🔾
14 🔾
Moll de Mestral
Moll de Gregal
Port Olímpic

H

Pg de Circumval·lació
Ronda del Litoral
Av del Litoral
C de Trelawny
17 🌠
Ⓠ 15

Edifici de Gas Natural
Ⓞ 5
Pg de Salvat Papasseit

Parc de la Barceloneta
Pg Marítim de la Barceloneta

Platja de la Barceloneta

C d'Andrea Dòria
de Guiter
LA BARCELONETA
C de Sant Carles

de l'Almirall Cervera

13 🔾
Ⓠ 16

Platja de Sant Sebastià

Mediterranean Sea

atja de ant Miquel

🅝 0 ——— 400 m
0 ——— 0.2 miles

For reviews see
🔾	Sights	p78
🔾	Eating	p79
Ⓠ	Drinking	p82
🌠	Entertainment	p83
🔒	Shopping	p83

Sights

Museu d'Història de Catalunya
MUSEUM

1 Map p76, C3

From the caves of the Pyrenees to the air-raid shelters of the civil war, from prehistory to the present day, this well-presented and sometimes interactive display gives the Catalan version of how its people have ridden history's ups and downs. Pick up an English-language guide at reception and don't miss the view from the top-floor restaurant. (www.mhcat.net; Plaça de Pau Vila 3; adult/child under 7/senior/student €4/free/free/3, 1st Sun of month free; ⊘10am-7pm Tue & Thu-Sat, to 8pm Wed, to 2.30pm Sun; Ⓜ Barceloneta)

Transbordador Aeri
CABLE CAR

2 Map p76, D5

This cable car (aka *funicular aeri*), strung out precariously across the harbour to Montjuïc, provides a bird's-eye view of the city and a convenient way to get to the museums of Montjuïc. The cabins float between Miramar (Montjuïc) and the Torre de Sant Sebastià (La Barceloneta). (Passeig Joan de Borbó; one way/return €10/15; ⊘11am-8pm; Ⓜ Barceloneta)

La Rambla de Mar
WATERFRONT

3 Map p76, B5

The city's authorities extended the world-famous La Rambla thoroughfare out into the sea in the early 2000s, connecting the city with the reclaimed port area of Port Vell. Seeming to float above the water, it offers reasonable views of the waterfront.

L'Aquàrium
AQUARIUM

4 Map p76, C4

The 80m-long shark tunnel is the high point in this, one of Europe's largest aquariums. Some 11,000 fish (including about a dozen sharks) have become permanent residents here, in an area filled with 4.5 million litres of water. The restless sharks are accompanied by splendid flapping rays, huge sunfish and fish from most of the world's oceans. (www.aquariumbcn.com; Moll d'Espanya; adult/child/senior €18/13/15; ⊘9.30am-9.30pm; Ⓜ Drassanes)

Edifici de Gas Natural
NOTABLE BUILDING

5 Map p76, E2

While only 100m high, this shimmering glass waterfront tower (designed

Local Life
Harbourside Art 1

Designed by the American pop artist Roy Lichtenstein in 1992, the 14m **Barcelona Head** (Map p76, B3), just back from Port Vell at the end of Passeig de Colom, sparkles like a ceramic comic when the sun strikes its *trencadís* (broken-tile) coating. Most visitors walk past oblivious, but locals love it because the sculpture is believed to be a homage to Gaudí.

Barcelona Head sculpture by Roy Lichtenstein, Port Vell

by Enric Miralles) is extraordinary for its mirrored surface and weirdly protruding adjunct buildings, which could be giant glass cliffs bursting from the main tower's flank. (Passeig de Salvat Papasseit; M Barceloneta)

Museu Marítim

MUSEUM

 6 Map p76, A5

Much of Barcelona's medieval prosperity depended on sea trade. In these former Gothic shipyards you get a sense of the glory and adventure of that maritime history, from the era of rafts to the age of steam. At the time of research, the museum's permanent collection was closed for renovation, with only temporary exhibitions open. (www.mmb.cat, in Catalan & Spanish; Avinguda de les Drassanes; adult/child/concession €2.50/free/2; ☉10am-8pm; M Drassanes)

Eating

Suquet de l'Almirall

SEAFOOD €€

7 Map p76, D4

The order here is simply top-class seafood. House specialities include *arròs a la barca* (rice laden with fish, squid and tomato) and *suquet* (seafood stew). Another good option is the *pica pica marinera* (a seafood mix, €42). Although chef Quim Marqués once worked in the kitchens of elBulli (the multi-award-winning restaurant run by master chef Ferran Adrià), his touch is light. Book for lunch on Sunday. (☏93 221 62 33; www.suquetdelalmirall.com;

Understand

The Changing Fortunes of Catalonia

Catalan identity is a multifaceted phenomenon, but Catalans are, more than anything else, united by the collective triumphs and shared grievances of the region's tumultuous past.

The Catalan golden age began in the early 12th century when Ramon Berenguer III, who already controlled Catalonia and parts of southern France, launched the region's first seagoing fleet. In 1137 his successor, Ramon Berenguer IV, was betrothed to the one-year-old heiress to the Aragonese throne, thereby giving Catalonia sufficient power to expand its empire out into the Mediterranean. By the end of the 13th century, Catalan rule extended to the Balearic Islands and Catalonia's seaborne trade brought fabulous riches.

But storm clouds were gathering; weakened by a decline in trade and foreign battles, Catalonia was vulnerable. And when Fernando became king of Aragón in 1479 and married Isabel, Queen of Castile, Catalonia became a province of Castile. Catalonia resented its new subordinate status but could do little to overturn it. After backing the losing side in the War of Spanish Succession (1702–13), Barcelona rose up against the Spanish crown whose armies besieged the city from March 1713 until 11 September 1714. The victorious Felipe V abolished Catalan self-rule, built a huge fort (the Ciutadella) to watch over the city, banned writing and teaching in the Catalan language, and farmed out Catalonia's colonies to other European powers.

Trade again flourished from Barcelona in the centuries that followed, and by the late 19th and early 20th centuries there were growing calls for greater self-governance to go with the city's burgeoning economic power. However, after Spanish general Francisco Franco's victory in 1939, Catalan Francoists and the dictator's army shot in purges at least 35,000 people, most of whom were either anti-Franco or presumed to be so. Over time, the use of Catalan in public was banned, all street and town names were changed into Spanish, and Castellano Spanish was the only permitted language in schools and the media. Franco's lieutenants remained in control of the city until his death in 1975 and the sense of grievance in Barcelona remains even to this day, more than three decades after self-government was restored in Catalonia in 1977. You'll see this reflected in the near-universal use of Catalan in public, the prevalence of Catalan flags on many facades and a general revival in Catalan culture.

Passeig de Joan de Borbó 65; meals €45-50; ⏱lunch & dinner Tue-Sat, lunch Sun; Ⓜ Barceloneta)

Can Solé SEAFOOD €€

8 Map p76, D4

A block back from the waterfront, Can Solé does a splendid job of maintaining seafood traditions (it's been here since 1903) without engaging in too much modern frippery. It's a classy place with, unusually, an open kitchen. Our favourite order is a well-priced dish of *fideus a banda* (noodles in a fish broth). (☎93 221 50 12; www.cansole.cat; Carrer de Sant Carles 4; meals €35-45; ⏱lunch & dinner Tue-Sat, lunch Sun; Ⓜ Barceloneta)

Cheriff SEAFOOD €€

9 Map p76, D3

A prime candidate among locals for Barcelona's best paella restaurant, Cheriff has eclectic maritime decor and fabulous rice dishes. The *paella de marisco* (seafood paella) and *arroz bogavante* (lobster rice) are both outstanding, but it's the *arroz caldoso* (rice in a seafood broth) that wins our affections. (☎93 319 69 84; Carrer de Ginebra 15; meals €40-45; ⏱lunch & dinner Mon-Sat; Ⓜ Barceloneta)

Somorrostro MODERN CATALAN €€

10 Map p76, D3

This modern, designer eatery is a real find. Its exposed stone walls and modern look reflect its approach to cooking. The menu changes daily,

but at the time of research included anemone tempura, and *butifarra* (Catalan pork sausage) served with calamari. It's creative and yet somehow true to Catalan traditions. (☎93 225 00 10; www.restaurantesomorrostro.com; Carrer de Sant Carles 11; meals €25-45, set evening menu €16.50; ⏱dinner Mon & Wed-Sat, lunch & dinner Sun; Ⓜ Barceloneta)

Xiringuito d'Escribà SEAFOOD €€

11 Map p76, G1

The esteemed Escribà pastry family (see p41) serves up excellent seafood at this popular waterfront eatery beyond Port Olímpic. There are many reasons to come here, not least the fact that this is one of the few places where one person can order from the selection of paella and *fideuá* (Catalan noodle dish similar to paella) – there's usually a minimum of

Local Life
Old Barceloneta

Don't be put off by the irregular opening hours or run-down appearance, **La Cova Fumada** (Map p76, D4; Carrer de Baluard 56; ⏱9.30am-3.30pm Mon-Wed, 6-8.30pm Thu & Fri, 9.30am-2pm Sat; Ⓜ Barceloneta) is one of our favourite Barceloneta bars. It's the sort of place where youngsters jostle with been-coming-here-for-decades locals while bar staff shout orders to no one in particular. Order a beer, or a vermouth, the spicy potato *tapa* called *la bomba*, and enjoy the show.

two people. (☏93 221 07 29; www.escriba. es; Ronda Litoral 42, Platja de Bogatell; meals €40-50; ⏰lunch & dinner Mon-Sat, lunch Sun; Ⓜ Llacuna)

Torre d'Alta Mar MEDITERRANEAN €€€

12　⊗　Map p76, D5

The aerial views from the top of this metal tower make it the most spectacular dining setting in town. Seafood dominates the menu, the wine list is strong and the food and service are generally good. You'll find better elsewhere, but not in many places and certainly not with these views. It's the perfect spot for a special occasion. (☏93 221 00 07; www. torredealtamar.com; Torre de Sant Sebastià, Passeig de Joan de Borbó 88; meals €70-80; ⏰dinner Sun & Mon, lunch & dinner Tue-Sat; Ⓜ Barceloneta)

Local Life
Harbourside Art 2

American Rebecca Horn's striking sculptural tribute to La Barceloneta, **Homenatge a la Barceloneta** (Map p76, E4) is an eye-catching column of rusted-iron-and-glass cubes on Platja de Sant Sebastià.

Erected in 1992, it pays homage to the beach bars and restaurants that disappeared around the time of the Olympic Games, and hence it has earned the respect of even the crustiest local old-timers.

Can Majó SEAFOOD €€

13　⊗　Map p76, E4

Virtually on the beach (with tables outside in summer), Can Majó has been serving seafood since 1968 and is best known for its rice dishes (€15 to €22) and cornucopian *suquets* (fish stews). Some say that it's trading on its past glories, but we enjoyed the *calderó d'arròs amb llamàntol* (rice casserole with lobster served in broth). (☏93 221 58 18; Carrer del Almirall Aixada 23; meals €40-50; ⏰lunch & dinner Tue-Sat, lunch Sun; Ⓜ Barceloneta)

El Cangrejo Loco SEAFOOD €€

14　⊗　Map p76, G1

The 'Mad Crab' is the pick of the culinary crop at the Port Olímpic marina – it's invariably full. Such fish standards as *bacallá* (cod) and *rap* (monkfish) are served in various guises (the salted cod with honey is a particular surprise) and melt in the mouth, as does the *sarsuela,* a fish stew. Also offers tapas. (☏93 221 05 33; www.elcangrejoloco.com; Moll de Gregal 29-30; meals €35-50; ⏰lunch & dinner; Ⓜ Ciutadella Vila Olímpica)

Drinking

CDLC LOUNGE BAR

15　⊕　Map p76, F2

Seize the night at the Carpe Diem Lounge Club, where you can lounge in Asian-inspired surrounds. It's ideal for

Homenatge a la Barceloneta by Rebecca Horn

sip a summertime beer outside or cosy up for a coffee in winter at the tiny tables inside. (Carrer de Guitert 60; ⏰10.30am-7pm Sun-Mon & Wed-Thu, to 10pm Fri & Sat; Ⓜ Barceloneta)

Entertainment

Poliesportiu Marítim
THALASSOTHERAPY

17 ⭐ Map p76, F2

Water babies will squeal with delight in this thalassotherapeutic (sea-water therapy) sports centre. Apart from the smallish swimming pool, there's a labyrinth of hot, warm and freezing-cold spa pools, and thundering waterfalls for a wonderful massage. (www.claror.cat, in Catalan; Passeig Marítim de la Barceloneta 33-35; admission Mon-Fri €17.50, Sat & Sun €20; ⏰7am-midnight Mon-Fri, 8am-9pm Sat, 8am-4pm Sun; Ⓜ Ciutadella Vila Olímpica)

a slow warm-up to the evening, especially if you find yourself on one of the cushions. You can come for the food, or wait until about midnight when the tables are packed up and the DJs and dancers take over. (www.cdlcbarcelona.com; Passeig Marítim de Barceloneta 32; ⏰noon-3am; Ⓜ Ciutadella Vila Olímpica)

Santa Marta
BAR

16 🍺 Map p76, E4

Could-be-anywhere beachfront bars line the beach, but this take-it-easy, seaside bar was made for its young, travelling crowd – the kind who've chosen to hang out in Barcelona in search of themselves or until their pennies run out. Have a light meal,

Shopping

Maremàgnum
SHOPPING MALL

18 🔒 Map p76, C5

A busy mall on the water, Maremàgnum offers an assortment of shops, bars and eateries over several floors. At FC Botiga on the ground floor you'll find FC Barcelona shirts and other football souvenirs. Or perhaps sexy women's underwear at the Love Store is more your thing. The list is long! (www.maremagnum.es; Moll d'Espanya; ⏰10am-10pm; Ⓜ Drassanes)

Explore

Passeig de Gràcia & L'Eixample

L'Eixample, bisected by the monumental Passeig de Gràcia, is the sophisticated alter ego to Barcelona's old city. This is where Modernisme left its most enduring mark and it's here that some of the city's most iconic architectural landmarks reside. With elegant shops, terrific restaurants and pulsating nightlife, it all adds up to one of the city's most rewarding neighbourhoods.

The Sights in a Day

☀️ The earlier you get to **Casa Batlló** (p88) and **La Pedrera** (p86) the better your chances of avoiding a queue. If you linger over the weird-and-wonderful detail of these sites, you could easily spend a couple of hours in each, which should just leave time to admire **Casa Amatller** (p94) and get the lowdown on contemporary art at the **Fundació Antoni Tàpies** (p94).

☀️ Take a break from museums with a tapas crawl that takes in the full range of tapas traditions at **Tapaç 24** (p97), **Bar Mut** (p98) and **Casa Alfonso** (p98) followed by some shopping at **Vinçon** (p90), **Joan Murrià** (p102) and **Camper** (p102) among others. Finish off the afternoon at the **Museu del Modernisme Català** (p95).

🌙 L'Eixample nights can be long and liquid, but we suggest one last Modernista fling: dinner at **Restaurant Casa Calvet** (p98), with its otherwise-inaccessible Gaudí interiors. **Cosmo** (p91) is a great place to ease into the night, while **Bar Velódromo** (p100) is another favourite. Perhaps some live music at **Bel-luna Jazz Club** (p102), then it just has to be **Dry Martini** (p100).

For a local's day of shopping in L'Eixample, see p90.

Getting There

Ⓜ **Metro** Passeig de Gràcia (lines 2, 3 and 4) and Diagonal (lines 3, 5 and 7) are in the heart of L'Eixample.

Ⓜ **Metro** Around L'Eixample's perimeter are Catalunya, Universitat, Hospital Clínic, Verdaguer and Girona.

🚃 **FGC Trains** Provença and Passeig de Gràcia stations.

Top Sights
La Pedrera

One of the Passeig de Gràcia's, and indeed Barcelona's, most beautiful Modernista structures, La Pedrera – officially called Casa Milà after its owners, but nicknamed La Pedrera (The Stone Quarry) by bemused locals who watched Gaudí build it from 1905 to 1910 – is in the top tier of Gaudí's achievements. Conceived as an apartment block, its approach to space and to light and its blurring of the dividing line between decoration and functionality will leave you gasping at the sheer originality of it all.

⊙ Map p92, D2

http://obrasocial.caixa catalunya.cat

Carrer de Provença 261-265

adult/child/concession €14/free/10, audioguide €4

⊙9am-8pm

Ⓜ Diagonal

Chimneys on the roof of La Pedrera (Casa Milà)

Don't Miss

The Facade

The natural world was one of the most enduring influences on Gaudí's work, and La Pedrera's undulating grey stone facade evokes a cliff-face sculpted by waves and wind. The wave effect is emphasised by elaborate wrought-iron balconies that bring to mind seaweed washed up on the shore. The lasting impression is of a building on the verge of motion.

The Roof Terrace

Gaudí's blend of mischievous form with ingenious functionality is evident on the roof, with its clusters of chimneys, stairwells and ventilation towers that rise and fall atop the structure's wave-like contours like giant medieval knights. Some are unadorned; others are decorated with *trencadís* (ceramic fragments) and even broken *cava* bottles. The deep patios, which Gaudí treated like interior facades, flood the apartments with natural light.

Espai Gaudí

With 270 gracious parabolic arches, the Espai Gaudí (Gaudí Space) feels like the fossilised ribcage of some giant prehistoric beast. At one point, 12 arches come together to form a palm tree. Watch out also for the strange optical effect of the mirror and hanging sculpture on the east side. Otherwise, Espai Gaudí offers an overview of Gaudí's work.

La Pedrera Apartment

Below the attic, the apartment (El Pis de la Pedrera) spreads out. Bathed in evenly distributed light, twisting and turning with the building's rippling distribution, the labyrinthine apartment is Gaudí's vision of domestic bliss. In the ultimate nod to flexible living, the apartment has no load-bearing walls: the interior walls could thus be moved to suit the inhabitants' needs.

☑ Top Tips

▶ If you're visiting more Barcelona museums, consider buying ArticketBCN (see the boxed text, p49) for admission to this and six other museums for €25.

▶ La Pedrera is extremely popular: be waiting when the doors open at 9am to avoid the worst of the crowds.

▶ Given the choice, take the detailed (not general) audioguide, which costs the same and offers far better value for money.

✗ Take a Break

Just north of La Pedrera, across the Avenida Diagonal, Bar Mut (p98) is a lovely spot for tapas and a glass of wine as you plan your next Modernista excursion.

An excellent choice for lunch across the other side of the Passeig de Gràcia, Petit Comite (p98) does a classy three-course meal for €18.

Top Sights
Casa Batlló

If La Sagrada Família (p104) is Gaudí's master symphony, Casa Batlló is his whimsical waltz – not to mention one of the weirdest-looking concoctions to emerge from his fantastical imagination. From the playful genius of its facade to its revolutionary experiments in light and architectural form (straight lines are few and far between), Casa Batlló, which was built as an anything-but-humble apartment block, is one of the most beautiful buildings in this city where competition for such a title is fierce.

👁 Map p92, E3

www.casabatllo.es

Passeig de Gràcia 43

adult/child under 7/ concession €18.15/ free/14.55

🕙10am-9pm Tue-Sun

Ⓜ Passeig de Gràcia

Detail of the curved windows in Casa Batlló's facade

Don't Miss

The Facade

To Salvador Dalí it resembled 'twilight clouds in water'. Others see a more-than-passing resemblance to the Impressionist masterpiece *Water Lillies* by Claude Monet. A Rorschach blot for our imagination, Casa Batlló's facade is exquisite and fantastical, sprinkled with fragments of blue, mauve and green tiles, and studded with wave-shaped window frames and mask-like balconies.

Sala Principal

The staircase wafts you to the 1st floor, where everything swirls in the main salon: the ceiling twists into a whirlpool-like vortex around its sun-like lamp; the doors, window and skylights are dreamy waves of wood and coloured glass in mollusc-like shapes. The sense of light and space here is extraordinary thanks to the wall-length window onto Passeig de Gràcia.

Back Terrace

Opening onto an expansive L'Eixample patio, Casa Batlló's back terrace is like a fantasy garden in miniature. It's a place where flowerpots take on strange forms and where the accumulation of broken ceramic pieces (*trencadís*) – a mere 330 of them on the building's rear facade – has the effect of immersing you in a kaleidoscope.

The Roof

Casa Batlló's roof, with the twisting chimney pots so characteristic of Gaudí's structures, is the building's grand crescendo. The eastern end represents Sant Jordi (St George) and the Dragon; one local name for Casa Batlló is the *casa del drac* (house of the dragon). The ceaseless curves of coloured tiles have the effect of making the building seem like a living being.

☑ Top Tips

▸ Queues to get in are frequent and on occasion opening hours can be shortened, so try turning up early in the morning.

▸ Although Casa Batlló stays open until 9pm, the last entry tickets are sold at 8pm.

▸ Even if you've already visited, return after sunset to see the facade illuminated in all its glory.

✗ Take a Break

Two short blocks down the hill and just off the other side of Passeig de Gràcia, Tapaç 24 (p97) is one of Barcelona's most innovative tapas bars.

A short walk west of Casa Batlló, Alba Granados (p99) is a typical modern L'Eixample restaurant – great cooking and wines in a relaxed setting.

Local Life
Shopping in the Quadrat d'Or

While visitors to L'Eixample do the sights, locals go shopping in the Quadrat d'Or, the grid of streets either side of the Passeig de Gràcia. This is Barcelona at its most fashion- and design-conscious, which also describes a large proportion of L'Eixample's residents. All the big names are here, alongside boutiques of local designers who capture the essence of Barcelona cool.

....

❶ **Designer Barcelona**
It has a reputation as the essence of innovative Catalan design and the frame in which Spanish design evolves, but **Vinçon** (www.vincon.com; Passeig de Gràcia 96; ◷10am-8.30pm Mon-Sat; Ⓜ Diagonal) has its roots in L'Eixample and is a neighbourhood icon. Pamper your aesthetic senses with a journey through its household wares.

➋ The New Wave

You could spend an entire day along Passeig de Gràcia but detour for a moment to **Lurdes Bergada** (www.lurdesbergada.es; Rambla de Catalunya 112; ⏰10.30am-8.30pm Mon-Sat; Ⓜ Diagonal), a boutique run by mother-and-son designer team Lurdes Bergada and Syngman Cucala. The classy men's and women's fashions use natural fibres and have attracted a cult following.

➌ A Pastry Stop

Time for a break. And few pastry shops have such a long-established pedigree as **Mauri** (www.pasteleriasmauri.com; Rambla de Catalunya 102; ⏰8am-9pm Mon-Sat, 9am-3pm Sun; Ⓜ Diagonal). The plush interior is capped by an ornate fresco dating back to Mauri's first days in 1929. Its croissants and feather-light *ensaïmadas* (sweet buns) are near perfect.

➍ Father of Fashion

Once the outfitter of James Bond and now focusing on design, **Armand Basi** (www.armandbasi.com; Passeig de Gràcia 49; ⏰10am-8pm Mon-Sat; Ⓜ Passeig de Gràcia) is one of Barcelona's most respected fashion stalwarts. This stylish stalwart also does slinky numbers for women: uptown suits in black, evening wear, leather jackets and accessories.

➎ Modernista Jewellery

This is more than just any old jewellery store. The boys from **Bagués** (www.bagues.com; Passeig de Gràcia 41; Ⓜ Passeig de Gràcia) have been chipping away at precious stones and moulding metal

since the 19th century, and many of the classic pieces here have a flighty, Modernista influence. Bagués backs it up with service that can be haughty, but owes much to old-school courtesies.

➏ Fine Foods

Fine foods and drink are as important to L'Eixample's shoppers as fashion, which is why **Colmado Quilez** (Rambla de Catalunya 63; ⏰9am-2pm & 4.30-8.30pm Mon-Sat; Ⓜ Passeig de Gràcia) is a local institution. Wines, quality canned seafood and traditional Catalan foods ideal for taking home climb the walls behind the iconic window display.

➐ Fine Wines

It only opens in the afternoon during the week, but since 1981 **Xampany** (Carrer de València 200; ⏰4.30-10pm Mon-Fri, 10am-2pm Sat; Ⓜ Passeig de Gràcia), a 'cathedral of *cava*', has established itself as one of the area's best-loved shops. There are few more Catalan gifts to take home than *cava*, and this is an Aladdin's cave of the stuff, with bottles crammed high into every chaotic corner of this dimly lit locale.

➑ Chill Down

Cosmo (www.galeriacosmo.com; Carrer d'Enric Granados 3; ⏰10am-10pm Mon-Thu, noon-2am Fri-Sat, noon-10pm Sun; Ⓜ Universitat; 🛜) is a groovy space with psychedelic colours, high white walls for exhibitions, and a nice selection of teas, pastries and snacks. Set on a pleasant pedestrian strip, it's perfect for an evening tipple while admiring the art.

A **B** **C** **D**

1

C c'Alfons XII

C d'Aribau

Travessera de Gràcia

C de Tuset

C de Moià

Via Augusta

Plaça de Narcís Oller

C de Sèneca

Plaça de Joan Carles I

Diagonal Ⓜ

C de Bonavista

C de Còrsega

11 ⊗

Palau del Baró Quadras

C de Pau Claris

Fundació ◎7 Suñol

La Pedrera

2

Av Diagonal

C de Balmes

C d'Enric Granados

C del Rosselló

Provença Ⓜ

Diagonal Ⓜ

12 ⊗

Pg de Gràcia

Rambla de Catalunya

27 ⊕

28

18 ⊗

19 ⊗

L'ESQUERRA DE L'EIXAMPLE

Fundac Antoni Tàpie

3

C de Londres

C de Casanova

C de Villarroel

C de C de Paris

C de Còrsega

Plaça del Doctor Ferrer Cajigal

C d'Aribau

C de Muntaner

C de Mallorca

⊗16

Plaça del Doctor Letamendi

Museu del Modernisme Català

C d'Aragó

C d'Enric Granados

4

Ⓜ Hospital Clínic

C de Provença

C de Casanova

15⊗

14 ⊗

22 ⊗

21 ⊕

Universitat Barcelor

C del Rosselló

C del Comte d'Urgell

C de València

Plaça de Universita

Av de Roma

C d'Aragó

23 ⊗

C de la Diputació

C de Casanova

Gran Via de les Corts Catalanes

C de Sepúlveda

For reviews see

◉	Top Sights	p86
◎	Sights	p94
⊗	Eating	p96
⊕	Drinking	p100
⊕	Entertainment	p102
⊕	Shopping	p102

5

C del Comte Borrell

C del Consell de Cent

C de Villarroel

Urgell Ⓜ

Ronda

17 ⊗

Sights

Fundació Antoni Tàpies   MUSEUM

1 ⊙ Map p92, D3

This Lluís Domènech i Montaner building (considered by many to be the prototype for Modernisme, and the first in Barcelona to be built on an iron frame) houses the experimental work of Catalonia's greatest living artist, Antoni Tàpies, as well as exhibitions by other contemporary artists. The building is crowned with a curious Tàpies coiled-wire sculpture

 Top Tip

Modernisme Unpacked

Aficionados of Barcelona's Modernista heritage should consider the **Ruta del Modernisme** (www.rutadelmodernisme.com) pack. For €12 you receive a guide to 115 Modernista buildings great and small, a map and discounts of up to 50% on the main Modernista sights in Barcelona, as well as some in other municipalities around Catalonia. For €18 you get another guide and map, *Sortim*, which leads you to bars and restaurants located in Modernista buildings. Pick up the packs at one of three Centres del Modernisme: the main tourist office at Plaça de Catalunya 17-S, the Hospital de la Santa Creu i Sant Pau and the Pavellons Güell in Pedralbes.

titled *Núvol i Cadira* (Cloud and Chair). (www.fundaciotapies.org; Carrer d'Aragó 255; adult/concession €7/5.60; ⊙10am-7pm Tue-Sun; MPasseig de Gràcia)

Casa Amatller   NOTABLE BUILDING

2 ⊙ Map p92, E3

Casa Amatller, by Josep Puig i Cadafalch, has Gothic-style window frames, a stepped gable borrowed from the urban architecture of the Netherlands, and all sorts of unlikely sculptures and busts jutting out. The pillared foyer (open to the public) is like some romantic castle. Renovations due for completion in 2012 will see the 1st floor converted into a museum. (www.amatller.org; Passeig de Gràcia 41; admission free; ⊙10am-8pm Mon-Sat, 10am-3pm Sun; MPasseig de Gràcia)

Palau Montaner   NOTABLE BUILDING

3 ⊙ Map p92, E2

Interesting on the outside and made all the more enticing by its gardens, this creation by Lluís Domènech i Montaner is spectacular on the inside. Completed in 1896, its central feature is a grand staircase beneath a broad, ornamental skylight. The interior is laden with sculptures, mosaics and fine woodwork. (www.rutadelmodernisme.com; Carrer de Mallorca 278; adult/child €6/3; ⊙tours in English 10.30am Sat, in Catalan 11.30am Sat, 10.30am & 12.30pm Sun, or Spanish 12.30pm Sat & 11.30pm Sun; MPasseig de Gràcia)

Designer homewares at Vinçon (p90) in the Quadrat d'Or

Fundación Francisco Godia   MUSEUM

4 ⊙ Map p92, E3

An intriguing mix of medieval art, ceramics and Modernista paintings makes up this eclectic private collection. Its medieval works include Romanesque wooden statues of the Virgin and child, and there are paintings by such Catalan icons as Jaume Huguet and Valencia's Joaquín Sorolla. The collection is housed in the beautifully restored Modernista Casa Garriga Nogués. (Carrer de la Diputació 250; adult/child under 5/student €5.50/free/3.50; ⊙10am-8pm Wed-Mon; Ⓜ Passeig de Gràcia)

Museu del Modernisme Català   MUSEUM

5 ⊙ Map p92, D4

Housed in a Modernista building, the ground floor of this museum seems like a big Modernista furniture showroom. Several items by Antoni Gaudí, including chairs from Casa Batlló and a mirror from Casa Calvet, share space with some typically whimsical, mock-medieval pieces by Josep Puig i Cadafalch. The basement is lined with Modernista art. (www.mmcat. cat; Carrer de Balmes 48; adult/child/student €10/5/7; ⊙10am-8pm Mon-Sat, to 2pm Sun; Ⓜ Passeig de Gràcia)

Understand

Modernisme

In the late 19th century, Barcelona was booming and the city's culture of avant-garde experimentation was custom made for a group of outrageously talented architects who came to be known as Modernistas. Leading the way was Antoni Gaudí i Cornet (1852–1926). Gaudí personifies and largely transcends a movement that brought a thunderclap of innovative greatness to an otherwise middle-ranking European city.

Modernisme did not appear in isolation in Barcelona. To the British and French the style was art nouveau; the Germans called it Jugendstil (Youth Style). Whatever it was called, a key uniting element was the sensuous curve, implying movement, lightness and vitality. Modernista architects looked to the past for inspiration: Gothic, Islamic and Renaissance design in particular. At its most playful, Modernisme was able to intelligently flout the rule books of these styles and create exciting new cocktails.

The Architects

Gaudí and the two architects who most closely followed him in talent, Lluís Domènech i Montaner (1850–1923) and Josep Puig i Cadafalch (1867–1957), were Catalan nationalists. The political associations are significant, as Modernisme became a means of expression for Catalan identity; the style barely touched the rest of Spain.

Gaudí took great inspiration from Gothic styles, but he also sought to emulate the harmony he observed in nature. Straight lines were out. The forms of plants and stones were in. Gaudí used complex string models weighted with plumb lines to make his calculations. The architect's work is at once a sublime reaching-out to the heavens, and an earthy appeal to sinewy movement.

The Materials & Decoration

Stone, unclad brick, exposed iron and steel frames, and copious use of stained glass and ceramics in decoration, were all features of the new style. Modernista architects relied heavily on the skills of craftsmen who were the heirs of the guild masters and had absorbed centuries of know-how about working with these materials. There were no concrete pours. Gaudí in particular relied on the old skills and even ran schools in La Sagrada Família workshops in a bid to keep them alive. Newer materials, such as forged iron, also came into their own during this period.

Palau del Baró Quadras

NOTABLE BUILDING

6 Map p92, D1

Josep Puig i Cadafalch built Palau del Baró Quadras between 1902 and 1904, festooning the fantastical facade with neo-Gothic carvings and a fine stained-glass gallery. It houses Casa Asia, an Asia-Pacific cultural centre. Visiting the varied temporary exhibitions allows you to get a peek at the inside of this intriguing building, which is full of surprising oriental themes. (Avinguda Diagonal 373; ⊙10am-8pm Tue-Sat, to 2pm Sun; MDiagonal)

Fundació Suñol

MUSEUM

7 Map p92, D2

Rotating exhibitions within this private art collection offer some 1200 works in total, mostly from the 20th century. Here you'll find everything from the photography of Man Ray to sculptures by Alberto Giacometti, as well as works by a hefty band of Spanish artists, including Picasso and Jaume Plensa. (www.fundaciosunol.org; Passeig de Gràcia 98; adult/concession €5/3; ⊙4-8pm Mon-Sat; MDiagonal)

Casa de les Punxes

NOTABLE BUILDING

8 Map p92, E1

Josep Puig i Cadafalch created this neo-Gothic fantasy, built between 1903 and 1905 and looking more like a fairy tale castle than an apartment block. Officially the Casa Terrades,

the building's pointed turrets earned it the nickname Casa de les Punxes (House of Spikes). (Avinguda Diagonal 420; MVerdaguer)

Casa Calvet

NOTABLE BUILDING

9 Map p92, G3

Gaudí's first apartment block and most conventional building won him the only award of his life – the city council's prize for the best building of 1900. It's sober from the outside, but there are hints of whimsy in the ground-floor restaurant; try to catch a glimpse when the doors open. (Carrer de Casp 48; MUrquinaona)

Eating

Tapaç 24

TAPAS €€

10 Map p92, E3

Carles Abellán, master of Comerç 24 in La Ribera (p67), runs this delightful basement tapas haven, turning out gourmet versions of old faves. Specials

---

✓ Top Tip

Artco Ticket

If little-visited private collections of art are your thing, consider buying an **Artco Ticket** (€15), which grants entry to six such galleries, including the Fundación Francisco Godia (p95) and Fundació Suñol (p97). Tickets can be purchased at the six participating museums or online at www.barcelonaturisme.cat.

include the *bikini* (usually a toasted ham-and-cheese sandwich, but here the ham is cured and the truffle makes all the difference!) and a thick *arròs negre de sípia* (squid-ink black rice). (www.tapas24.net; Carrer de la Diputació 269; meals €30-35; ⊙9am-midnight; Ⓜ Passeig de Gràcia)

Bar Mut   TAPAS €€

11 Map p92, D1

The tapas here get rave reviews from Barcelona's knowledgeable food critics. Cured meats and surprising combinations are what this place is all about. The menu, chalked up on a blackboard in Spanish, includes top-notch seafood from a can, a Catalan tradition. Ask the waiter to help you put together an order. (Carrer de Pau

Local Life
Carrer d'Enric Granados

Half the city's population would like to live on Carrer d'Enric Granados (Map p92, D4). The pedestrianised end, at Carrer de la Diputació, is marked off by the **gardens** (⊙10am-sunset Mon-Fri from Plaça de l'Universitat, 10am-sunset Sat & Sun from Carrer de la Diputació) of the Universitat de Barcelona. The banter of diners can be heard at nearby restaurants as you wander rows of elegant apartments to the leafy Plaça del Doctor Letamendi. From here, one lane of traffic trickles along until you reach Avinguda Diagonal (this end is also pedestrian only).

Claris 192; meals €30-35; ⊙11am-midnight Mon-Sat, noon-5pm Sun; Ⓜ Diagonal)

Petit Comite   CATALAN €€

12 Map p92, D2

The food in this sophisticated eatery on a L'Eixample back lane takes the culinary traditions of Catalonia, from hearty Pyrenean stews to seafood-rich rice dishes, and nudges them in subtle new directions. Try the pigs' trotters with plums or the meatballs with squid. The three-course 'la barra express' (€18) is one of the neighbourhood's best bargains. (www.petitcomite. cat; Passatge de la Concepció 13; meals €45-50; ⊙lunch & dinner Tue-Sun; Ⓜ Diagonal)

Casa Alfonso   MEDITERRANEAN €

13 Map p92, G3

In business since 1934 and a veritable museum of period interiors, Casa Alfonso is perfect for a tapas stop at the long marble bar. Timber-panelled and festooned with old photos, posters and swinging hams, it attracts a faithful local clientele for its *flautas* (thin custom-made baguettes with your choice of filling), hams, cheeses, hot dishes and homemade desserts. (www.casaalfonso.com; Carrer de Roger de Llúria 6; meals €20-25; ⊙9am-1am Mon-Sat; Ⓜ Urquinaona)

Restaurant Casa Calvet   MEDITERRANEAN €€€

A top-end and top-notch Barcelona experience, Restaurant Casa Calvet is set on the ground floor of Gaudí-designed

Casa Calvet (see 9 ⊙ Map p92, G3). This classy place draws an upmarket crowd for creative Mediterranean cooking with a Catalan bent and a menu that changes with the seasons. Savour Gaudí's architectural genius as you enjoy your partridge with chestnuts. (☎93 412 40 12; www.casacalvet.es; Carrer de Casp 48; meals €60-70; ⊙lunch & dinner Mon-Sat; ⓂUrquinaona)

Cinc Sentits
CATALAN €€

14 ✕ Map p92, C4

Almost universally praised by critics and the proud bearer of a Michelin star, the 'Five Senses' blends originality (yes, there are the famous foams of molecular gastronomy) with tradition based around the freshest and highest-quality ingredients (Costa Brava seafood or suckling pig from the Spanish interior). If it could just turn down the lighting, the whole experience would be perfect. (☎93 323 94 90; www.cincsentits.com; Carrer d'Aribau 58; meals €55-65; ⊙lunch & dinner Tue-Sat, closed Aug; ⓂPasseig de Gràcia)

Cata 1.81
TAPAS €€

15 ✕ Map p92, C4

Treat yourself to a series of dainty gourmet dishes, such as *raviolis amb bacallá, humus, ceps i tomàquets* (salt-cod ravioli with hummus, mushrooms and tomato) or *macarrons amb sobrassada i xocolata blanca* (macaroni with tangy Mallorcan pork-paprika sausage and white chocolate). The waiters know their wines and

CARLES ALLENDE/TAPAÇ 24 ©

Fresh ingredients on display at Tapaç 24 (p97)

there's a long list to choose from. A good option is one of the various tasting menus. (www.cata181.com; Carrer de València 181; meals €40-50, set menus €30-46; ⊙dinner Mon-Sat, closed Aug; ⓂPasseig de Gràcia)

Alba Granados
MEDITERRANEAN €€

16 ✕ Map p92, C3

Fresh tastes, great wines, terrific desserts and a base in traditional Spanish and Catalan cooking make for a winning combination at this attractive restaurant. We liked the sardine tartar with foie gras and apple almost as much as the romantic tables for two on the 1st-floor balcony. (Carrer d'Enric Granados 34; meals €35-45; ⊙lunch & dinner Mon-Sat, lunch Sun; ⓂDiagonal)

Bodega La Sepúlveda   CATALAN €€

17 🍴 Map p92, D5

The range of dishes in this classic Catalan eatery is a little overwhelming, mixing traditional choices (cold meats, cheeses and Catalan faves like *cap i pota,* a dish of chunks of fatty beef in gravy) with more surprising options like *carpaccio de carbassó amb bacallà i parmesà* (thin zucchini slices draped in cod and parmesan cheese). (www.bodegasepulveda.net; Carrer de Sepúlveda 173; meals €25-30; ⊙lunch & dinner Mon-Fri, dinner Sat; MUniversitat)

Drinking

Bar Velódromo   BAR, CAFE

18 🍷 Map p92, A2

This historic L'Eixample classic (said to have served as the unofficial headquarters of the Republican government during the Spanish Civil War) reopened its doors in 2009 after a 10-year hiatus. It's back to its best: lofty ceilings, terrific tapas, ice-cold Moritz beer and an atmosphere that never misses a beat, from your early morning coffee to an end-of-night *mojito*. (Carrer de Muntaner 213; ⊙6am-3am; MDiagonal)

Dry Martini   COCKTAIL BAR

19 🍷 Map p92, B2

For decades this has been one of the city's great cocktail joints, a classic of discreet, white-jacketed waiters who will whip up a fine, well, dry martini, or any other cocktail fantasy. Sit at the bar or plunge into the bloated leather lounges. (www.drymartinibcn.com; Carrer d'Aribau 162-166; ⊙5pm-3am; MDiagonal)

Les Gens Que J'Aime   BAR

20 🍷 Map p92, E2

Incurably romantic, this basement bar is an intimate relic of the 1960s, combining jazz in the background, candlelight and privacy with antique red-velvet sofas and dark-wood furniture and trims. It's the perfect place for a night of sweet nothings. (Carrer de València 286; ⊙6pm-2.30am Sun-Thu, to 3am Fri & Sat; MPasseig de Gràcia)

Local Life
A Grand Old Cafe

If you're out beyond the eastern side of the Passeig de Gràcia, step a century back in history by stepping into the **Cafè del Centre** (Map p92, F2; Carrer de Girona 69; ⊙8am-midnight Mon-Fri; MGirona). It's an atmospheric place that's been in business since 1873.

A timber-topped bar extends down the right side as you enter, fronted by a slew of marble-topped tables and dark timber chairs. Out the back is an old piano. This cafe exudes an almost melancholy air but gets busy at night.

DIEGO LEZAMA/LONELY PLANET IMAGES ©

Barman mixing cocktails at Dry Martini

La Chapelle

BAR

 21 Map p92, C4

A typical, long, narrow L'Eixample bar with white-tiled walls like a 1930s hospital. It's replete with religious decor – a plethora of crucifixes and niches that far outdoes what you'd find in any other 'chapel'. This is a relaxed gay meeting place that welcomes all. (Carrer de Muntaner 67; ⏰6pm-2am Mon-Thu, to 3am Fri & Sat; Ⓜ Universitat)

Dietrich Gay Teatro Café

CABARET

22 Map p92, C4

A classic of the Gaixample, this place hosts some of the best drag in the city in its elegant quarters – all-timber

finishing on two levels. Quiet during the week, it goes a little wild with drag shows, acrobats and dancing from Friday on. (Carrer del Consell de Cent 255; ⏰10.30pm-3am; Ⓜ Universitat)

Antilla BCN

CLUB

23 Map p92, B5

The salsateca in town, this is the place to come for Cuban *son,* merengue, salsa and a whole lot more. If you don't know how to dance any of this, you may feel a little silly (as a bloke) but will probably get free lessons (if you're a lass). The guys can come back at another time and pay for lessons. (www.antillasalsa.com, in Spanish; Carrer d'Aragó 141; ⏰11pm-6am; Ⓜ Urgell)

Entertainment

Bel-luna Jazz Club
LIVE MUSIC

24 ⭐ Map p92, E4

This basement establishment is not the prettiest location but attracts a full nightly program of contemporary jazz with a diversion into the blues for a jam session on Mondays. It draws local and visiting acts and kicks off around 10.30pm. When the last act finishes, it turns into a club playing 1980s and '90s tunes. (www.bel-luna.com, in Spanish; Rambla de Catalunya 5; admission €5-15; ⏰9pm-2am Sun-Thu, to 3am Fri & Sat; MCatalunya)

Shopping

Joan Murrià
FOOD & DRINK

25 🔒 Map p92, E2

This superb grocer-delicatessen has been run by the same family since the early 1900s and continues to showcase the culinary wonders of Catalonia and beyond. Inspect the eye-catching facade, featuring original designs by Modernista painter Ramon Casas. (www.murria.cat; Carrer de Roger de Llúria 85; ⏰9am-2pm & 5-8.30pm Tue-Fri, 10am-2pm & 5-8.30pm Sat; MPasseig de Gràcia)

Cacao Sampaka
FOOD

26 🔒 Map p92, E3

Chocoholics will be convinced they have died and passed on to a better place. Load up in the shop (look for zany-but-somehow-just-right combinations that, for example, combine chocolate with balsamic vinegar) or head for the bar where you can have a classic *xocolata calenta* (hot chocolate). (www.cacaosampaka.com; Carrer del Consell de Cent 292; ⏰9am-9pm Mon-Sat; MPasseig de Gràcia)

Camper
SHOES

27 🔒 Map p92, D2

This classic Mallorcan shoe merchant stamps all over the international market by successfully treading the fine line between rebellion and commercialism. Its original line in bowling-shoe chic has evolved, now ranging from the eminently sensible to the stylishly fashionable. There are several branches in town. (www.camper.com; Carrer de València 249; MPasseig de Gràcia)

El Bulevard dels Antiquaris
ANTIQUES

28 🔒 Map p92, D3

Part of the Bulevard Rosa shopping arcade, this stretch is crammed with around 70 antique shops tempting you with the 'this and thats' of times gone by. A few of the specialist shops to look out for include Brahuer (jewellery) and Victor i Fills (crystal). (www.bulevarddelsantiquaris.com; Passeig de Gràcia 55-57; ⏰10.30am-8.30pm Mon-Sat; MPasseig de Gràcia)

Chocolates on display at Cacao Sampaka

Regia
PERFUME

29 Map p92, E3

Regarded as one of the best perfume stores in the city, Regia stocks all the name brands and has a private perfume museum out the back. It also sells creams, lotions, colognes and bath products. (www.regia.es, in Catalan & Spanish; Passeig de Gràcia 39; ☺9.30am-8.30pm Mon-Fri, 10.30am-8.30pm Sat; Ⓜ Passeig de Gràcia)

Loewe
ACCESSORIES

Loewe is one of Spain's leading and oldest fashion icons – it was founded in Madrid in 1846. This branch close to Regia (see **29** Map p92, E3) specialises in luxury leather, including shoes, accessories and travel bags. It also has lines in perfume, sunglasses, cufflinks, silk scarves and jewellery. It opened in 1943 in the Modernista Casa Lleó Morera. (www.loewe.es; Passeig de Gràcia 35; ☺10am-8.30pm Mon-Sat; Ⓜ Passeig de Gràcia)

Adolfo Domínguez
FASHION

30 Map p92, E3

This Galician chain is one of Spain's most celebrated fashion stores. Designs are classic and a little conservative but all in timeless good taste for men, women and kids, with exquisite tailoring and quality materials. This branch is enormous. (www.adolfodominguez.com; Passeig de Gràcia 32; Ⓜ Passeig de Gràcia)

Top Sights
La Sagrada Família

Getting There

M Metro The Metro is the easiest way to arrive, via Sagrada Família station (lines 2 and 5).

Walking La Sagrada Família is an easy 1.5km walk from Passeig de Gràcia.

Spain's biggest tourist attraction and a work in progress for more than a century, La Sagrada Família is a unique, extraordinary piece of architecture. Conceived as a temple as atonement for Barcelona's sins of modernity, this giant church became Gaudí's holy mission. When completed it will have a capacity for 13,000 faithful and is, in medieval fashion, a work of storytelling art. Rich in religious iconography and symbolism, at once ancient and thoroughly modern, La Sagrada Família leaves no one unmoved.

La Sagrada Família in summer

Don't Miss

Nativity Facade

This astonishing tapestry in stone is, for now, the single most impressive feature of La Sagrada Família. Step back for an overall sense of this remarkable work, which was the first of the facades completed (in 1930), then draw near to examine the detail. It is replete with sculpted figures (Gaudí used plaster casts of local people as models) and images from nature.

Passion Facade

Symbolically facing the setting sun, the Passion Facade – stripped bare and left to speak for itself – is the austere counterpoint to the Nativity Facade's riotous decoration. From the Last Supper to his burial, Christ's story plays out in an S-shaped sequence from bottom to top. Check the cryptogram in which the numbers always add up to 33, Christ's age at crucifixion.

Glory Facade

The Glory Facade will be the most fanciful of them all, with a narthex boasting 16 hyperboloid lanterns topped by cones that will look something like an organ made of melting ice cream. Gaudí made only general drawings of the facade, but its symbolism is clear: Christ in all His glory and the road to God.

Main Nave

In the main nave, the heart of the temple's sanctuary, pay particular attention to the columns (Gaudí used trees as inspiration), the absence of flat surfaces, and the apse (one of the earliest features to be completed) capped by pinnacles that hint at the genius Gaudí later deployed elsewhere in the church.

www.sagrada familia.org

Carrer de Mallorca 401

adult/child/concession €12.50/free/10.50, audioguide €4

⊙ 9am-8pm

☑ Top Tips

▶ Jump the queue by booking tickets in advance at ServiCaixa (www.servicaixa.com).

▶ The Nativity Facade is lit up from dusk to midnight.

▶ The best time to visit is at opening time on weekdays.

✕ Take a Break

It's not often we recommend Irish pubs, but **Michael Collins Pub** (Plaça de la Sagrada Família 4; ⊙ noon-2am Sun-Thu, to 3am Fri & Sat; Ⓜ Sagrada Família) is an unusually authentic version of the genre. Better still, you'll find more locals here than foreigners.

Crypt

From the main apse, holes in the floor allow a view down into the crypt, which was the first part of the church to be completed in 1885. Built in a largely neo-Gothic style, it's here that Gaudí lies buried. The crypt has often been used as the main place of worship while the remainder of the church is completed.

Side Nave & Nativity Transept

The side nave, inside the door that leads beneath the Nativity Facade, is stunning with Doric-style columns and stained-glass windows. It's primarily worth visiting for the view of the main nave and its forest of columns, and of the inside of the Nativity Facade. Most people rush through here and miss one of the best interior views.

Bell Towers

The towers of the three facades represent the 12 Apostles (so far, eight have been built). Lifts whisk visitors up one tower of the Nativity and Passion Facades (the latter gets longer queues) for marvellous views. There will be 18 towers – 12 Apostles, four evangelists, the Virgin Mary and Christ – which when completed will make this the world's tallest church building.

Museu Gaudí

Jammed with old photos, drawings and restored plaster models that bring Gaudí's ambitions to life, the museum also houses an extraordinarily complex plumb-line device he used to calculate his constructions. It's like journeying through the mind of the great architect. Some of the models are upside down, as that's how Gaudí worked to best study the building's form and structural balance.

Organ

In 2010 a 1492-pipe organ was finally installed in the church's presbytery. So vast is the acoustic space the organ needs to serve that further organs will later be added around the sanctuary; these will either be playable separately or all together from the one keyboard, with an estimated 8000 pipes in all.

Nearby: Hospital de la Santa Creu i Sant Pau

A masterpiece of Modernista style, the **Hospital de la Santa Creu i Sant Pau** (www.santpau.es; Carrer de Sant Antoni Maria Claret 167; Ⓜ Hospital de Sant Pau) is a short 500m walk north of La Sagrada Família. Designed by Lluís Domènech i Montaner and completed by his son in 1930, its highlights are the 16 lavishly decorated pavilions.

Understand
Antoni Gaudí

- -

Antoni Gaudí i Cornet (1852–1926) was born in Reus, trained initially in metalwork and obtained his architecture degree in 1878. Among his first works were rather modest lamp posts for Barcelona's Plaça Reial (p34). His first big break came when a showcase he designed for a glove manufacturer for the 1878 World Fair in Paris so impressed industrialist Eusebi Güell that he commissioned Gaudí for Palau Güell (p49) and Park Güell (p110) among other projects. In 1883, with a growing reputation, Gaudí took over the project on which he would work for the next 43 years – La Sagrada Família.

Although he joined (and came to personify) the Modernista movement, Gaudí had a style all his own. A recurring theme was his obsession with the harmony of natural forms. With age he became almost exclusively motivated by stark religious conviction and from 1915 he gave up all other projects to devote himself to La Sagrada Família. In doing so, he is said to have remarked: 'My good friends are dead. I have no family and no clients, no fortune nor anything. Now I can dedicate myself entirely to the Church.'

The main themes of Gaudí's work are also evident in La Pedrera (p86) and Casa Batlló (p88), which are a riot of the unnaturally natural, or the naturally unnatural. Not only are straight lines eliminated, but the lines between real and unreal, sober and dream-drunk are all blurred. The grandeur of his vision was matched by an obsession with detail, as evidenced by his use of *trencadís* constructed from discarded ceramic pieces.

Gaudí spent his last 12 years preparing plans for the completion of La Sagrada Família. When he died in June 1926 – he was knocked down by a tram on Gran Via de les Corts Catalanes, mistaken for a vagrant and died three days later in the Antic Hospital de la Santa Creu i Sant Pau (p50) – less than a quarter of La Sagrada Família had been completed. It is unlikely to be finished before 2026. As Gaudí is reported to have said when questioned about the never-ending project, 'My client is not in a hurry'.

Local Life
Village Life in Gràcia

Getting There

☉ Gràcia is a downhill walk from Park Güell.

Ⓜ **Metro** Fontana station (line 3) or Joanic (line 4).

🚃 **FGC Trains** Gràcia station is on the neighbourhood's western edge.

Located halfway between L'Eixample and Park Güell, Gràcia was a separate village until 1897 and its tight, narrow lanes and endless interlocking squares maintain a unique, almost village-like identity to this day. In places bohemian, in others rapidly gentrifying, Gràcia is Barcelona at its most eclectic, its nooks and crannies home to everything from sushi bars to badly lit old taverns.

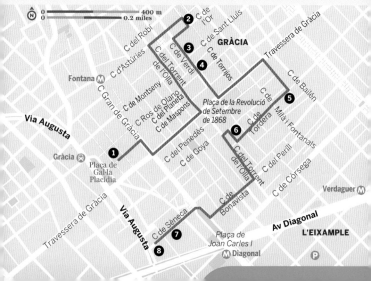

❶ Local Market

Built in the 1870s and covered in fizzy Modernista style in 1893, the **Mercat de la Llibertat** (Plaça de la Llibertat; ☉8am-8.30pm Mon-Fri, to 3pm Sat; ℝFGC Gràcia) is a market emblematic of the Gràcia district – full of life and fresh produce. Its architect was Francesc Berenguer i Mestres (1866–1914), Gaudí's long-time assistant.

❷ Plaça de la Virreina

Thanks to the low-slung houses (built for the low-wage workers from Gràcia's textile factories) along one side and the 17th-century Església de Sant Joan on the other, Plaça de la Virreina is one of the most village-like of Gràcia's squares. It's a hub for locals and has outdoor tables around the perimeter.

❸ Urban Fashion

Carrer de Verdi is one of Gràcia's most enticing streets. Home to an art-house cinema and a colourful series of bars and restaurants, it's also filled with little fashion boutiques – a Gràcia speciality. For urban wear and accessories, stop in **Red Market** (Carrer de Verdi 20; ☉5-9.30pm Mon, 11.30am-2pm & 5-9.30pm Tue-Sat; Ⓜ Fontana)

❹ Local Bar

Especially welcoming in winter, **Bar Canigó** (Carrer de Verdi 2; ☉5pm-2am Mon-Thu, to 3am Fri & Sat; Ⓜ Fontana) is a corner bar on an animated square and a timeless locals' spot to sip on Estrella beer around rickety tables and indulge in some banter. There's also a pool table.

❺ Catalan Tradition

Catalan families in high spirits pile into **Cal Boter** (Carrer de Tordera 62; ☉lunch & dinner Tue-Sun; Ⓜ Joanic) for piles of local grub, such as the curious *mar i muntanya* (surf and turf) combination of *bolets i gambes* (mushrooms and prawns). The atmosphere is of a simpler age. A few tables are scattered in the leafy little backyard.

❻ Gràcia's Tavern

If you like your taverns unchanged for years, with huge old wine barrels and a motley crew of punters, from local guzzlers to grungy Erasmus students, **Raïm** (www.raimbcn.com; Carrer de Progrés 48; ☉8pm-2.30am; Ⓜ Diagonal) could be for you. It has wall-to-wall photos of Cuba, and the *mojitos* here are excellent.

❼ New-Wave Shopping

Nobodinoz (www.nobodinoz.com; Carrer de Sèneca 9; ☉10.30am-2.30pm & 4.30-8.30pm Mon-Sat; Ⓜ Diagonal) claims to be Spain's first concept store for kids. The range of toys, clothes, furnishings and knick-knacks drifts from vintage to chic and is all about the new Gràcia.

❽ Scandinavian Design

The gentrification of southern Gràcia isn't just for kids. **Snö Mito Nórdico** (Carrer de Sèneca 33; ☉10.30am-2.30pm & 4.30-8.30pm Mon-Sat; Ⓜ Diagonal) brings the best in Nordic fashions – think achingly cool and crisp lines – to Barcelona, as well as stunning home accessories as only the Scandinavians can make them.

Top Sights
Park Güell

Getting There

M Metro The walk to the park is signposted from both Vallcarca and Lesseps stations (both line 3).

🚌 Bus Bus 24 drops you at an entrance near the top of the park.

One of Antoni Gaudí's best-loved creations, Park Güell – a fantasy public park that was designed as a gated playground for Barcelona's rich – climbs a hillside north of the centre. This is where the master architect turned his hand to landscape gardening and the result is an expansive and playful stand of greenery interspersed with otherworldly structures glittering with ceramic tiles. The lasting impression is of a place where the artificial almost seems more natural than the natural.

Gaudí's characteristically fluid lines and *trencadís* decorations, Park Güell

Carrer d'Olot 7

admission free

🕙 10am-9pm

Don't Miss

Stairway & Sala Hipóstila

The steps up from the entrance and the two *Hansel and Gretel*–style gatehouses are a mosaic of fountains, ancient Catalan symbols and a much-photographed dragon-lizard. Atop the stairs is the Sala Hipóstila, a forest of 86 Doric columns (some of them leaning at an angle and all inspired by ancient Greece); the space was intended as a market.

Banc de Trencadís

Atop the Sala Hipóstila is a broad open space; its highlight is the Banc de Trencadís, a tiled bench curving sinuously around the perimeter and alternately interpreted as a mythical serpent or, typically for Gaudí, waves in the sea. Although Gaudí was responsible for the form, the *trencadís* (broken tile) surface designs were the work of Gaudí's right-hand man, Josep Maria Jujol.

Casa-Museu Gaudí

The spired house east of the Banc de Trencadís is the **Casa-Museu Gaudí** (www.casamuseugaudi.org; adult/child/concession €5.50/free/4.50; 🕙10am-8pm), where Gaudí lived for most of his last 20 years (1906–26). It contains furniture by him and other memorabilia, and its muted interior is a curious contrast to the extravagance of so many of the structures he designed.

The Viaducts

Much of the park's eastern end is dominated by the viaducts, which were Gaudí's solution to the problem of getting people and vehicles (not water) into the park. Slanting columns and local stone create an astonishing effect, seeming to spring from a fairy tale and creating the illusion that the whole structure was carved out of the mountain itself.

☑ **Top Tips**

▶ If travelling by Metro, Vallcarca station is better for arriving (the uphill trek to the park is eased by escalators); Lesseps is better for leaving (it's downhill all the way).

▶ Study the details: crockery pieces adorn some sections of the Banc de Trencadís.

▶ Arrive early on weekdays and avoid weekends in summer.

✗ **Take a Break**

Around 1km southeast down the hill from the park entrance is **La Panxa del Bisbe** (Carrer de Rabassa 37; 🕙lunch & dinner Tue-Sat; M Joanic), a highly recommended (and well-priced) gourmet tapas haunt.

Explore

Montjuïc & Poble Sec

Watching over sea and city from on high, Montjuïc is a lovely stand of green and gardens interspersed with wonderful museums and sites that took centre stage during the 1992 Olympics. At the foot of the hill, a world away in Poble Sec, the tightly packed streets are home to an engaging collection of bars and tapas haunts.

The Sights in a Day

☼ Before we get started, a word of warning: food on the hill is generally overpriced, so pack a picnic lunch from the Mercat de la Boqueria (p44). However you get here – we suggest the Transbordador Aeri cable car (p78) from Barceloneta – take the funicular up to the summit and work your way down. The **Castell de Montjuïc** (p122) promises marvellous views, as do the **Jardins del Mirador** (p123). Spend a couple of hours at the **Fundació Joan Miró** (p118) before finding a quiet corner of the **Jardins de Mossèn Cinto de Verdaguer** (p123) for lunch.

☼ Spend a couple of hours at the **Museu Nacional d'Art de Catalunya** (p114), and with what's left of your time we recommend you head for **L'Anella Olímpica & Estadi Olímpic** (p122), then **Poble Espanyol** (p122) and **Fundació Fran Daurel** (p122), before descending to see what's happening at **CaixaForum** (p122).

☾ Stay long enough to catch **La Font Màgica** (p125) before heading on to **Quimet i Quimet** (p125) and **Celler Cal Marino** (p126) for great tapas, followed by a drink at **Tinta Roja** (p126).

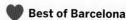

◉ Top Sights

Museu Nacional d'Art de Catalunya (p114)

Fundació Joan Miró (p118)

♥ Best of Barcelona

Museums

Museu Nacional d'Art de Catalunya (p114)

Fundació Joan Miró (p118)

CaixaForum (p122)

Poble Espanyol (p122)

Fundació Fran Daurel (p122)

Museu Olímpic i de l'Esport (p123)

Museu d'Arqueologia de Catalunya (p123)

Museu Etnològic (p125)

Refugi 307 (p125)

Getting There

Ⓜ **Metro & Funicular** Paral·lel station (lines 2 and 3), then funicular railway (9am to 10pm) to Estació Parc Montjuïc (PM), where a cable car (*telefèric*) heads higher.

🚌 **Bus** Bus 50, 55 and 61, or No 193 from Plaça d'Espanya to the *castell* (castle).

🚠 **Cable Car** Transbordador Aeri (p78) from Torre de Sant Sebastiá in La Barceloneta to Montjuïc.

Top Sights
Museu Nacional d'Art de Catalunya

Barcelona's finest art collection looks out over the city from the Palau Nacional, the pompous centrepiece of the 1929 World Exhibition. The outrageously rich collection commences with a breathtaking selection of Romanesque art from the Pyrenees, and ends with a handful of works by Picasso and Dalí, with lavish detours into Gothic, Renaissance and baroque styles en route. Although there are many remarkable artworks here, it's the sheer breadth and scale of the collection that lives longest in the memory.

◉ Map p120, C3

www.mnac.es

Mirador del Palau Nacional

adult/child/senior/ concession €8.50/free/ free/6

🕙10am-7pm Tue-Sat, to 2.30pm Sun

Ⓜ Espanya

The exterior of Palau Nacional

Don't Miss

Romanesque Frescoes
The beautifully displayed Romanesque art section constitutes one of Europe's greatest such collections. It consists mainly of 11th- and 12th-century frescoes from churches in the Catalan Pyrenees. While it's all exceptional, the two outstanding collections are the Església de Sant Climent de Taüll frescoes (Room 7) and the Església de Santa Maria de Taüll frescoes (Room 9).

Gothic Altarpieces
Lovers of medieval religious art will want to linger over the rich ground-floor display of Gothic art, which is dominated by deeply textured altarpieces and other works, including paintings by Catalan painters Bernat Martorell and Jaume Huguet. Amid it all, seek out the sculpture *Head of Christ* by Jaume Cascalls, a haunting bust dating from 1352.

El Greco & Fra Angelico
Before leaving the Gothic centuries and heading upstairs, two paintings warrant close and prolonged inspection. The first is *Saint Peter and Saint Paul* (1595–1600) by Doménikos Theotokópoulos, better known as El Greco. The second work is the *Madonna of Humility* (1433–35) by Fra Angelico, an idealised, near-perfect counterpoint to El Greco's slender, elongated figures.

Spanish Masters
After passing through the soaring auditorium, climb to the 1st floor, where the masters of 17th-century Spanish art make a brief appearance. Francisco de Zurbarán's *Immaculate Conception* (1632) looks out across Room 39 at his strangely disconcerting *Saint Francis of Assisi*.

☑ **Top Tips**

▶ If you're visiting more Barcelona museums, consider buying ArticketBCN (see the boxed text, p49), which gives admission to this and six other museums for €25.

▶ Pick up the museum's free *Guide to the Visit* brochure, which highlights 35 masterpieces and their locations in the museum, but don't restrict yourself to these works alone.

✕ **Take a Break**

The cafe at the top of the steps near the entrance is fine for a coffee and a snack.

Down the hill and to the east along Avinguda del Paral·lel, Tickets (p126) is the latest project of Ferran Adrià, with tapas masterpieces in miniature, though you'll need to book ahead.

Museu Nacional d'Art de Catalunya

Ground Floor

Madonna of Humility
by Fra Angelico

Saint Peter &
Saint Paul
by El Greco

Església de Santa
Maria de Taüll
Frescoes

Església de Sant
Climent de Taüll
Frescoes

Gothic
Altarpieces

Exit   Entrance

Head of Christ
by Jaume Cascalls

Cafe

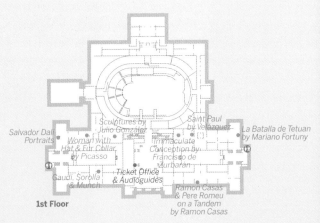

1st Floor

Salvador Dalí
Portraits

Sculptures by
Julio González

Woman with
Hat & Fur Collar
by Picasso

Saint Paul
by Velázquez

Immaculate
Conception by
Francisco de
Zurbarán

La Batalla de Tetuan
by Mariano Fortuny

Gaudí, Sorolla
& Munch

Ticket Office
& Audioguides

Ramon Casas
& Pere Romeu
on a Tandem
by Ramon Casas

Nearby, Room 41 is shared by Josep de Ribera and the masterful *Saint Paul* by Velázquez (1619).

Catalan Masters

The first floor is dominated by Catalan painters and offers an intriguing insight into artists little known beyond Catalonia. There's much to turn the head but our highlights are Mariano Fortuny's *La Batalla de Tetuan* (1863–73) and the works of Modernista painter Ramon Casas (1866–1932), especially *Ramon Casas and Pere Romeu on a Tandem* (1897).

Gaudí, Sorolla & Munch

Some furniture pieces by Antoni Gaudí and Joaquim Mir (1873–1940) continue the Catalan theme in Room 66 – the latter's *Terraced Village* (1909) is a lovely work. But dropped down amid this relatively uniform collection of Catalan art are two works by undoubted European masters: Valencian painter Joaquín Sorolla and Norwegian Edvard Munch.

Picasso & Dalí

Two sober works by Salvador Dalí – *Portrait of my Father* (1925) and *Portrait of Joan Maria Torres* (1921) – are what everyone comes to see in Room 73, but fans of Picasso are rewarded by a handful of paintings, among them the cubist *Woman with Hat and Fur Collar* (1937), which is one of the museum's standout pieces.

Julio González

Having checked off the big names, most visitors head for the exit, but we recommend you stay long enough to appreciate the beautiful sculptures by Julio González (1876–1942), Catalonia's premier 20th-century sculptor. His abstract human forms, such as those in *Still Life II* (1929), have a slender grace.

Top Sights
Fundació Joan Miró

Dedicated to one of the greatest artists to emerge in Barcelona in the 20th century, Joan Miró (1893–1983), this outstanding gallery is a must-see. The foundation holds the greatest single collection of the artist's work, comprising around 220 of his paintings, 180 sculptures, some textiles and more than 8000 drawings. Only a smallish portion is ever on display, but there's always a representative sample from his early paintings through to a master in full command of his unique style.

👁 Map p120, E3

www.bcn.fjmiro.es

Plaça de Neptu

adult/child €9/6, audioguide €4

🕐10am-8pm Tue-Wed, Fri-Sat, 10am-9.30pm Thu, 10am-2.30pm Sun

🚌50, 55, or 🚠funicular

Entrance to Fundació Joan Miró, Montjuïc

Don't Miss

The Formative Years
ROOM 16

The young Joan Miró began, like most masters, by painting figurative forms, but his move to Paris in 1920 prompted a shift to the avant-garde styles that he would make his own. His 1925 work *Painting (The White Glove)* has that unmistakable Miró sense of the artist having taken everything apart and reassembled on a whim.

The War Years
ROOM 17

Miró spent most of the Spanish Civil War (1936–39) in exile in France, and his works from this period are uncharacteristically dark. During WWII, his approach to painting changed, reflecting a desire to escape reality, as highlighted in the bold colours and childlike figures of *The Morning Star* (1940) and *Woman Dreaming of Escape* (1945).

1960s & Paper
ROOMS 19 & 20

After soaking up the vivid colours of Miró's 1960s paintings in Room 19 – linger over *Painting (for Emil Fernandez Miró)* from 1963 and *Catalan Peasant in the Moonlight* (1968) in particular – pause in Room 20. This is where Miró's love of painting on paper, and the flexibility it offered, is showcased with paintings that span five decades.

Col·lecció Katsuta
ROOMS 21 & 22

This far-reaching private collection of Miró's works feels like an unexpected bonus at exhibition's end. It's a reprise of his career from the sober Catalan landscapes of his youth (such as *Landscape, Mont-Roig* in Room 21) through to the masterful and enigmatic *The Smile of a Tear* (1973) in Room 22.

☑ Top Tips

▶ If you're visiting more Barcelona museums, consider buying ArticketBCN (see the boxed text, p49) for admission to this and six other museums for €25.

▶ Don't miss the basement *Homenatge a Joan Miró* (Homage to Joan Miró), with works by Henry Moore, Antoni Tàpies and Eduardo Chillida.

▶ Pay for the audioguide – it's worth every euro.

✗ Take a Break

There's a small cafe selling snacks in the museum – it's nothing special but you're not spoiled for choice in Montjuïc.

One of our favourite tapas bars in Barcelona, Quimet i Quimet (p125) is close to the bottom of the funicular station down in Poble Sec.

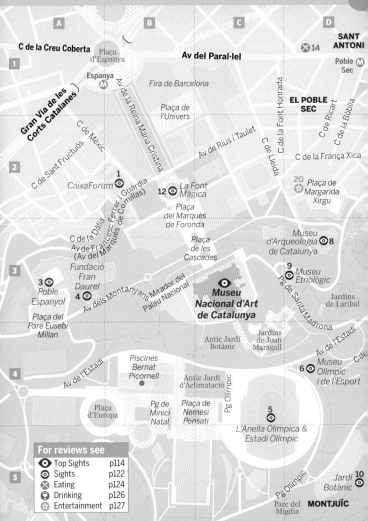

A **B** **C** **D**

SANT ANTONI

C de la Creu Coberta

Plaça d'Espanya

Av del Paral·lel

14

Poble Sec M

1

Espanya M

Fira de Barcelona

C de la Font Honrada

EL POBLE SEC

C de Ricart

C de la Bòbila

Gran Via de les Corts Catalanes

C de Mèxic

Av de la Reina Maria Cristina

Plaça de l'Univers

Av de Rius i Taulet

C de la França Xica

C de Lleida

C de Sant Fructuós

2

CaixaForum **1**

C de Francesc Ferrer i Guàrdia (Av del Marquès de Comillas)

12 La Font Màgica

Plaça del Marquès de Foronda

20 Plaça de Margarida Xirgu

Museu d'Arqueologia de Catalunya **8**

C de la Dàlia

Av de Francesc Ferrer i Guàrdia (Av del Marquès de Comillas)

Plaça de les Cascades

9 Museu Etnològic

3

Fundació Fran Daurel

Poble **3** Espanyol

4

Av dels Montanyans

Mirador del Palau Nacional

Pg de Santa Madrona

Jardins de Laribal

Plaça del Pare Eusebi Millan

Museu Nacional d'Art de Catalunya

Antic Jardí Botànic

Jardins de Joan Maragall

Av de l'Estadi

Museu **6** Olímpic i de l'Esport

4

Av de l'Estadi

Piscines Bernat Picornell

Antic Jardí d'Aclimatació

Pg Olímpic

C de

Plaça d'Europa

Pg de Minici Natal

Plaça de Nemesi Ponsati

5 L'Anella Olímpica & Estadi Olímpic

Jardí **10** Botànic

5

Pg Olímpic

MONTJUÏC

Parc del Migdia

For reviews see	
Top Sights	p114
Sights	p122
Eating	p124
Drinking	p126
Entertainment	p127

E F G H

Av del Paral·lel

0   400 m
0   0.2 miles

Parc de
les Tres
Xemeneies

Ⓜ Paral·lel

🌟 19

18

13

17

C de Vila i Vilà

C de Palaudàries

C de Radas
C de la Concòrdia

C de Blasco de Garay

C de Margarit

C de Blai

C de la Creu dels Molers

16

Plaça
del
Sortidor

15

C del Poeta Cabanyes

C de Tapioles

C del Roser

C de Salvà

C de Blesa

C de Cabanes

C de Piquer

C d'Annibal

Pg de l'Exposició

C Nou de la Rambla

C de la Fontrodona

Pg de Montjuïc

Miramar

11

Refugi 307

Pg de la Font Trobada

Plaça de
Carlos
Ibáñez

Plaça de
l'Armada

Pg de Miramar

Av de Miramar

C de Montjuïc

Jardins
de Miramar

Jardí de les
esculptures

**Fundació
Joan Miró**

Av de Miramar

Estació
Parc
Montjuïc

Plaça
de Dante

Jardins de
Joan Brossa

Gardens

7

Jardins de
Mossèn Costa
i Llobera

Plaça
de Neptu

Jardins de
Mossèn Cinto
de Verdaguer

Plaça de
la Sardana

Estació
Mirador

C de Montjuïc

Ctra de Miramar

Ctra de Miramar

es Pins

C del Doctor Font i Quer

Jardins
del
Mirador

Camí Baix del Castell

Av del Castell

Ronda del Litoral

Estació
del Port

Moll
de la
Costa

Pg del Migdia

Castell

C de la Cartoixa

**Castell de
Montjuïc**

2

Camí del Mar

Sights

CaixaForum
MUSEUM

1 Map p120, B2

An outstanding brick caprice by Modernista architect Josep Puig i Cadafalch, this building has been transformed by the Caixa building society from factory and cavalry barracks into one of Barcelona's best art spaces. Two or three separate exhibitions – either from the bank's extensive collection of modern art or a visiting exhibition – are on display at any one time. (www.fundacio.lacaixa. es; Avinguda de Francesc Ferrer i Guàrdia 6-8; admission free; ⏱10am-8pm Mon-Fri, to 9pm Sat & Sun; Ⓜ Espanya)

Castell de Montjuïc
CASTLE

2 Map p120, F5

Castell de Montjuïc dominates the southeastern heights of Montjuïc and enjoys commanding views over the Mediterranean. Make the charming walk along the base of the seaward walls along the Camí del Mar (a dirt trail), drinking in views of city and sea. Plans are afoot for an international peace centre in the castle and a display on its history. (⏱9am-9pm; 🚌PM, 🚠telefèric)

Poble Espanyol
CULTURAL AREA

3 Map p120, A3

The so-called Spanish Village, Poble Espanyol is both a cheesy souvenir-hunters' haunt and an intriguing scrapbook of Spanish architecture. Built for the Spanish crafts section of the 1929 exhibition, it's composed of plazas and streets lined with surprisingly good copies of characteristic buildings from across the country's regions. (www.poble-espanyol.com; Avinguda del Marquès de Comillas 13; adult/child/concession €9.50/5.60/6.60; ⏱9am-8pm Mon, to 2am Tue-Thu, to 4am Fri, to 5am Sat, to midnight Sun; Ⓜ Espanya, 🚌50, 61)

Fundació Fran Daurel
MUSEUM

4 Map p120, A3

Next to Poble Espanyol, this foundation is an eclectic collection of 300 works of art including sculptures, prints, ceramics and tapestries by modern artists ranging from Picasso and Miró to more contemporary figures, including Miquel Barceló. (www.fundaciofrandaurel.com; admission free; ⏱10am-7pm; Ⓜ Espanya, 🚌50, 61)

L'Anella Olímpica & Estadi Olímpic
OLYMPIC SITE

5 Map p120, C4

L'Anella Olímpica (Olympic Ring) is the group of installations built for the main events of the 1992 Olympics. They include the **Piscines Bernat Picornell**, where the swimming and diving events were held and the surprisingly small 65,000-capacity Estadi Olímpic, which is open to the public when it's not in use for sporting events or concerts. (Avinguda de l'Estadi; admission free; ⏱10am-8pm Apr-Sep; 🚌50, 61 or PM)

Castell de Montjuïc stands high above the city

Museu Olímpic i de l'Esport
MUSEUM

6 ⦿ Map p120, D4

Just over the road from the Olympic stadium, this sports museum is an interactive and visual smorgasbord of sporting history. It's centred on Olympic history but delves into anything from Formula 1 racing to the development of cricket under the British Raj. (www.fundaciobarcelona olimpica.es; Avinguda de l'Estadi; adult/child/senior/student €4/free/free/2.50; ☉10am-8pm Wed-Mon; ⧉50, 61 or PM)

Gardens
GARDENS

7 ⦿ Map p120, G3

The **Jardins del Mirador** offer fine views over the port of Barcelona. Fur-ther downhill, the **Jardins de Mossèn Costa i Llobera** are of particular interest for their collection of tropical and desert plants – including a forest of cacti. The beautiful, cool **Jardins de Mossèn Cinto de Verdaguer** are devoted to bulbs and aquatic plants. (☉10am-sunset; ⧉50 or PM)

Museu d'Arqueologia de Catalunya
MUSEUM

8 ⦿ Map p120, D3

This archaeology museum features artefacts discovered in Catalonia and Mediterranean Spain, from copies of pre-Neanderthal skulls to jewel-studded Visigoth crosses and Roman finds from Barcelona. It also houses a statue of a splendidly endowed, and

Understand
20th-Century Masters

Spain, and Catalonia in particular, produced an astonishing number of world-renowned 20th-century painters, but three stand high above the rest: Pablo Picasso, Salvador Dalí and Joan Miró.

Pablo Picasso
Born in Málaga in southern Spain, Pablo Ruiz Picasso (1881–1973) moved with his family to Barcelona in 1895. Despite spending much of his later life away from the city he returned often, and frequently said he considered Barcelona to be his true home. Picasso must have been one of the most restless artists of all time. His work underwent repeated revolutions as he passed from one creative phase to another – from his gloomy Blue Period, through the brighter Pink Period, and by the mid-1920s to dabbling with surrealism. Picasso went on to become the master of cubism, inspired by his fascination with primitivism, such as that of African masks and early Iberian sculpture. View a fine selection of his early works in Barcelona's Museu Picasso (p56).

Salvador Dalí
Separated from Picasso by barely a generation, Salvador Dalí (1904–89) started off dabbling in cubism, but quickly became identified with the surrealists. This complex character's 'hand-painted dream photographs', as he called them, are virtuoso executions brimming with detail and nightmare images dragged up from a feverish and Freud-fed imagination. Preoccupied with Picasso's fame, Dalí built himself a reputation as an outrageous showman and self-promoter. A frequent visitor to Barcelona, he was born in Figueres and spent much of his life in the seaside village of Cadaqués.

Joan Miró
Barcelona-born Joan Miró (1893–1983) developed a joyous and childlike style that earned him the epithet 'the most surrealist of us all' from the French writer André Breton. His later and best-known period is characterised by the simple use of bright colours and forms in combinations of symbols that represented women, birds (the link between earth and the heavens), stars (the unattainable heavenly world and source of imagination) and a sort of net that entraps all these levels of the cosmos. Fundació Joan Miró (p118) houses the most complete collection of his work.

aroused, Priapus (the god of male procreative power). You will find some rooms shut as the museum is slowly being overhauled. (www.mac.es; Passeig de Santa Madrona 39-41; adult/child/senior/student €3/free/free/2.10; ☻9.30am-7pm Tue-Sat, 10am-2.30pm Sun; 🚌55, 193)

Museu Etnològic   MUSEUM

9 ◉ Map p120, D3

The permanent exhibition, Ètnic, has several thousand wide-ranging items on show in three themed sections: Orígens (Origins), Pobles (Peoples) and Mosaics. Along with lots of material from rural areas of Catalonia and other parts of Spain, the museum's collections include items from Australia, Japan and Morocco. (www.museuetnologic.bcn.cat; Passeig de Santa Madrona 16-22; adult/child/concession €3.50/free/1.75; ☻noon-8pm Tue-Sat, 11am-3pm Sun; 🚌55)

Jardí Botànic   GARDENS

10 ◉ Map p120, D5

South across the road from the Estadi, this botanic garden was created atop an old municipal dump. The theme is 'Mediterranean' flora and the collection includes some 1500 species (40,000 plants) thriving in areas with a climate similar to that of the Mediterranean, from Spain to Turkey, Australia to South Africa and California to Chile. (www.jardibotanic.bcn.es; Carrer del Doctor Font i Quer 2; adult/child/student €3.50/free/1.70, 3-8pm Sun free; ☻10am-8pm; 🚌50, 61 or PM)

Refugi 307   HISTORIC SITE

11 ◉ Map p120, G2

Barcelona was the city most heavily bombed from the air during the Spanish Civil War and it was dotted with more than 1300 air-raid shelters. This one is a warren of low, narrow tunnels that was slowly extended as the war dragged on. The half-hour tours (in Catalan or Spanish; book ahead for English or French) explain how it worked. (☎93 256 21 22; www.museuhistoria.bcn.cat, in Catalan & Spanish; Carrer Nou de la Rambla 169; admission €3; ☻tours 10am-2pm Sat & Sun; Ⓜ Paral·lel)

La Font Màgica   FOUNTAIN

12 ◉ Map p120, B2

Delightfully over the top, the biggest of Montjuïc's famous fountains splashes into life with an irresistible 15-minute summer-evening extravaganza filled with music and light. Whether it's to the music of Tchaikovsky or ABBA, you'll be mesmerised by the waterworks. (Avinguda de la Reina Maria Cristina; ☻every half-hour 9.30-11.30pm; Ⓜ Espanya)

Eating

Quimet i Quimet   TAPAS €€

13 🍴 Map p120, F1

This postage-stamp-sized tapas bar is a gourmet paradise in miniature. Cram into this bottle-lined space for gourmet tapas, fine wine and even a specially made dark Belgian beer. Let the bar staff combine a few canapés, seafood tapas from a can or whatever's going. The *montadito de salmon* (salmon, cream cheese and honey) is exquisite. (Carrer del Poeta Cabanyes 25; meals €25-30; ⏱lunch & dinner Mon-Fri, lunch Sat; Ⓜ Paral·lel)

41° & Tickets
TAPAS €€

14 Map p120, D1

Tickets is the new venture of the celebrated Adrià brothers, Ferran and Albert, and it's easily the most exciting new tapas haunt in town – imagine grilled mini quails with honey and mint, or liquid ravioli with Cádiz cheese. Next door, 41° is an oh-so-sleek cocktail bar run by the same owners, where bar snacks include lime-and-coconut marshmallows. Reservations for both are essential. (☎93 292 42 54; www.ticketsbar.es; Avinguda del Paral·lel 164; ⏱dinner Tue-Fri, lunch & dinner Sat; Ⓜ Poble Sec)

La Tomaquera
SPANISH & CATALAN €

15 Map p120, E2

It's first in, first seated in this great local eatery, where waiters move like rockets delivering dishes of hearty grub and carafes sloshing with wine. Try the house speciality of snails or the *cassola de cigales* (a crayfish hotpot). It doesn't take credit cards. (Carrer de Margarit 58; meals €20-25; ⏱lunch & dinner Tue-Sat; Ⓜ Poble Sec)

Celler Cal Marino
TAPAS €€

16 Map p120, E2

This casual little wine bar does thoughtfully chosen tapas (including cheeses and quality canned Spanish seafood), as well as a range of terrific wines by the glass. If you bring a bottle, they'll even fill it for you to take home. (www.cellercalmarino.com; Carrer de Margarit 54; meals €45-55; ⏱lunch & dinner Mon-Fri, lunch Sat & Sun; Ⓜ Poble Sec)

Elche
CATALAN €€

17 Map p120, G1

Some places are just good at what they do and keep doing it. Hidden away from the old town centre, this old-style restaurant has been serving up a variety of paellas, rice dishes and *fideuà* (similar to paella but made with vermicelli noodles) since the 1960s. (Carrer de Vila i Vilà 71; meals €30-40; ⏱lunch & dinner; Ⓜ Poble Sec)

Drinking

Tinta Roja
BAR

18 Map p120, E1

Through a succession of tunnel-like spaces all suffused with reddish light, you penetrate to an area where anything could happen, from theatre to tango or acrobatics. The hushed atmosphere is always pleasant for a tipple. (Carrer de la Creu dels Molers 17; ⏱8.30pm-2am Thu, to 3am Fri & Sat; Ⓜ Poble Sec)

La Terrrazza
CLUB

Some of the biggest international names play at this summertime must, which can be relied on for a range of the meatiest house, techno-trance and pop-rock on vinyl, and a clientele of extremely high-quality eye candy. It all takes place under the stars inside the Poble Espanyol complex. (see 3 ◉ Map p120, A3; www.laterrrazza.com, in Spanish; Avinguda del Marquès de Comillas; admission €18; ⊙midnight-5am Thu, to 6am Fri & Sat May-Sep; Ⓜ Espanya)

Entertainment

Sala Apolo
LIVE MUSIC, CLUB

19 ⭐ Map p120, G1

This former music hall is the scene of a fiery and eclectic dance and concert venue. Gigs (often starting about 9pm) range from world music to touring rock bands you'll never again see in a venue so cosy. After the encores, the hall is cleared for clubbing (a DJ team plays house, electro and more). (www.sala-apolo.com; Carrer Nou de la Rambla 113; admission €7-22; ⊙12.30-6am Wed-Sat, 10.30pm-3.30am Sun; Ⓜ Paral·lel)

Tablao de Carmen
FLAMENCO

Named after the great *barcelonin bailaora* (flamenco dancer) Carmen Amaya, this place in Poble Espanyol (see 3 ◉ Map p120, A3) features a lively show with a full cast of guitarists,

DIEGO LEZAMA/LONELY PLANET IMAGES ©

Tapas at Quimet i Quimet (p125), Poble Sec

singers and dancers. It's touristy, but the quality is reasonable nonetheless. (☎93 325 68 95; www.tablaodecarmen.com; Carrer dels Arcs 9; show & drink €35, with tapas/dinner €45/69; ⊙shows 7.30pm & 10pm Tue-Sun; Ⓜ Espanya)

Teatre Mercat de les Flors
THEATRE

20 ⭐ Map p120, D2

At the foot of Montjuïc, this is an important venue for contemporary dance. The box office opens one hour before the show. (www.mercatflors.org; Carrer de Lleida 59; admission €15-20; ⊙box office 11am-2pm & 4-7pm Mon-Fri; Ⓜ Espanya)

Explore

Camp Nou, Pedralbes & Sarrià

The Camp Nou, home of FC Barcelona, is one of the greatest sporting temples on earth and a touchstone of Catalan identity. Up the hill to the north, village-like Sarrià belongs to a very different Barcelona. It's a refined, upmarket *barrio* (neighbourhood) that bears little resemblance to the touristy downtown area. Nearby Pedralbes is similar, and home to some fine museums.

The Sights in a Day

☼ Like most Barcelona attractions, the **Camp Nou** (p130) is a popular spot, so begin early at the stadium to be able to visit the stadium and museum in relative peace. A longish walk uphill takes you to the **Museu de Ceràmica** (p133), then continue uphill (you may want to hail a cab) for lunch at **Bar Tomàs** (p133).

☼ You could easily spend a couple of hours exploring **Old Sarrià** (see the boxed text, p135), with another hour at least to enjoy the **Museu-Monestir de Pedralbes** (p133). All this walking will have you clamouring for some fine foods for the journey – make sure you allow time for a visit to **Foix de Sarrià** (p135), **Semon** (p135) and **Oriol Balaguer** (p135).

☾ It's worth checking out who's playing at **Bikini** (p134), but if that doesn't appeal consider some oysters at **Gouthier** (p133) instead. The rest of the night could last long into the next morning if you choose to spend it at **Elephant** (p134).

  Top Sights

Camp Nou & the Museu del FC Barcelona (p130)

♥ **Best of Barcelona**

Eating
Gouthier (p133)
Bar Tomàs (p133)

Drinking & Live Music
Elephant (p134)
Bikini (p134)

Shopping
Foix de Sarrià (p135)
Oriol Balaguer (p135)

Getting There

Ⓜ **Metro** Collblanc station (line 5) is best for the Camp Nou.

🚃 **FGC Trains** The easiest way to get to Sarrià (Sarrià and La Bonanova stations) and the Museu-Monestir de Pedralbes (Reina Elisenda) is by suburban train from Catalunya station in the city centre.

Ⓜ **Metro** Palau Reial station (line 3) is the best option for reaching several museums in Pedralbes.

Top Sights
Camp Nou & the Museu del FC Barcelona

FC Barcelona, the world's most successful football club, plays at the Camp Nou, a stadium well matched with the grandeur of the team's achievements. Built in 1957 and enlarged for the 1992 World Cup, the stadium holds 99,000 people and is one of the world's largest. The stadium and club are also essential pillars in understanding how Catalans see themselves. To learn what all the fuss is about, come see a game, visit the museum or take a stadium tour.

Map p132, B4

www.fcbarcelona.com

Carrer d'Aristides Maillol

tickets €15-200, tours adult/child €22/16.50

10am-8pm Mon-Sat, to 2.30pm Sun

M Collblanc

FC Barcelona competes against Inter Milan at Camp Nou

Don't Miss

A Real, Live Game

Tours of an empty stadium are one thing, but there's nothing like turning up to watch Barça strut their stuff live. Buying tickets is possible online (www.servicaixa.com or www.ticketmaster.es), at outlets of Carrefour or FNAC, by phone (☎902 189900, or 93 496 36 00 outside Spain) or at the **Camp Nou ticket office** (Gate 14; ⏰9am-5pm Mon-Thu, 9am-2.30pm Fri, 9am-1.30pm Sat on home match days).

Museum

FC Barcelona's recently overhauled museum has a high-tech interactive mural, audiovisual displays and an astonishing collection of FC Barcelona memorabilia, from trophies (of which there are quite a few) to displays on the history of the club. Intriguingly, there are exhibits that highlight the four core values of FC Barcelona: Catalan identity, universality, social commitment and democracy.

Dressing Rooms & Pitch

The stadium tour takes you from the dressing room (sit where Lionel Messi psyches himself up before a game), and out onto the hallowed turf itself. Occupying the same space that so many footballing greats have graced with their presence is inspiration enough for many, but there's also the sheer scale of this place once you step onto the pitch...

The President's Box

Looking over it all from the president's box (part of the tour) offers another startling perspective on the Camp Nou. It's an epic place, populated with the ghosts of great sporting moments past, and it's here that, every year, the presidents of Barcelona and Real Madrid are forced to sit alongside one another to watch their teams do battle.

☑ Top Tips

▶ Tickets for matches are highly sought-after, but tickets for big matches are near-impossible to find, so choose matches against teams in the lower reaches of La Liga.

▶ Don't buy tickets from scalpers – prices are ridiculously high and there's high security around the stadium.

▶ Tours don't operate on match days and the museum may not be open.

▶ If you have a ticket for a game, get there well before kick-off to soak up the atmosphere and to make sure you find your seat in this vast stadium.

✕ Take a Break

There are plenty of bars in the vicinity of the stadium – joining the old timers propping up the bar in one of them, especially on match day, is an essential part of the Barcelona experience.

Sights

Museu-Monestir de Pedralbes

MONASTERY & MUSEUM

1 Map p132, A2

This peaceful museum provides an absorbing insight into medieval monastic life. Founded in 1326, the convent is a Catalan Gothic jewel with a three-storey cloister. Around the cloister, visit the restored refectory, kitchen, stables, stores and infirmary. Built into the cloister walls are day cells where the nuns spent most of their time in prayer and devotional reading. (www.museuhistoria.bcn.cat; Baixada del Monestir 9; Museu d'Història de Barcelona combined ticket adult/child/ concession €7/free/5; ☉10am-5pm Tue-Fri, to 7pm Sat, to 8pm Sun; 🚊FGC Reina Elisenda, 🚌22 or 64)

Museu de Ceràmica

MUSEUM

2 Map p132, A3

Welcome to perhaps the most fragile exhibition in Barcelona, an exceptional collection of Spanish ceramics dating from medieval times right up to the present day. Items on show include pieces by Miró and Picasso, as well as a charming selection of tiles depicting Catalan life. (www. museuceramica.bcn.es; Avinguda Diagonal 686; adult/concession €5/3, 1st Sun of month free; ☉10am-6pm Tue-Sun; Ⓜ Palau Reial)

Eating

Via Veneto

CATALAN €€€

3 Map p132, D3

Dalí regularly waltzed into this high-society eatery after it opened in 1967. The vaguely art-deco setting, orange-rose tablecloths, leather chairs and fine cutlery may cater to more conservative souls, but the painter was here for the kitchen exploits. Catalan dishes dominate the menu and they're mouth-wateringly good. (🕿93 200 72 44; www.viavenetorestaurant. com; Carrer de Ganduxer 10; meals €90-120; ☉lunch & dinner Mon-Fri, dinner Sat; 🚊FGC La Bonanova)

Gouthier

SEAFOOD €€

4 Map p132, C2

This sophisticated oyster bar – the first of its kind in Barcelona – captures the essence of Sarrià, serving up fresh French oysters as well as a range of exclusive French products (such as foie gras, smoked eel and monkfish liver). Choose well from an excellent wine list and you could find yourself in heaven. (www.gouthier.es; Carrer de Mañé i Flaquer 8; ☉lunch & dinner Tue-Sat, lunch Sun; 🚊FGC Sarrià)

Bar Tomàs

TAPAS €

5 Map p132, B2

Many *barcelonins* have long claimed that Bar Tomàs serves the city's best *patates braves* (roast potatoes with a slightly spicy tomato sauce), prepared

Cloister at the 14th-century Monestir de Pedralbes (p133)

here with a special variation on the traditional spicy tomato and mayonnaise sauce. The place is a rough-edged bar, but that doesn't stop the well-off citizens of Sarrià piling in, particularly for lunch on weekends. (Carrer Major de Sarrià; meals €15-20; ⏰lunch & dinner Thu-Tue; ℝFGC Sarrià)

Drinking

Elephant
CLUB

6 🔇 Map p132, B3

If you can manage to turn up here in a convertible, so much the better. Still one of Barcelona's better clubs, Elephant is like being invited to a celeb's garden party. Inside the big tent-like dance space things can heat up musically as the night wears on, but plenty of people just hang in the gardens with their cocktails. (www.elephantbcn.com; Passeig dels Tillers 1; admission Fri & Sat €15; ⏰11pm-3am Wed, to 5am Thu-Sun; Ⓜ Palau Reial)

Entertainment

Bikini
LIVE MUSIC

7 ⭐ Map p132, D3

Three main spaces define Bikini, one of the grand old stars of the Barcelona nightlife scene. Every possible kind of music gets a run, depending on the space you choose and the night. From Latin and Brazilian hip-jigglers to 1980s disco, from funk to hip-hop, it all happens here. Concerts usually start from 9pm, and when they're done it's DJs till dawn. (www.bikinibcn.com; Carrer de Déu i Mata 105; admission €10-20; ☺9pm-6am Wed-Sat; Ⓜ Maria Cristina)

Shopping

Foix de Sarrià
FOOD & DRINK

8 🔒 Map p132, B1

Since 1886 this exclusive pastry shop has been selling exquisite cakes and sweets. You can take them away or head out the back to sip tea, coffee or hot chocolate while sampling little cakes and other wizardry. (www.foixdesarria.com; Plaça de Sarrià 12-13; ☺8am-8pm Mon-Sat; ⓇFGC Reina Elisenda)

Semon
FOOD & DRINK

9 🔒 Map p132, D2

It's impossible to not be tempted by this upmarket deli, which is one of the most respected purveyors of fine foods in the city. This place is all about top brands of caviar, smoked salmon and cured meats, and there's an in-store cafe for those times when you can't wait to try it all. (www.semon.es; Carrer de Ganduxer 31; ☺10am-2.30pm & 5-9pm Mon-Wed, 10am-9pm Thu-Sat; ⓇFGC La Bonanova)

Oriol Balaguer
FOOD & DRINK

10 🔒 Map p132, D2

Pastry chef Oriol Balaguer worked in the kitchens of perhaps Spain's most celebrated chef, Ferran Adrià, in Catalonia and won the prize for

Ⓠ Local Life
A Wander Through Old Sarrià

Hugging the left flank of thundering Via Augusta (Map p132, C1), the old centre of Sarrià is a largely pedestrianised haven of peace. Probably founded in the 13th century and only incorporated into Barcelona in 1921, ancient Sarrià is formed around sinuous Carrer Major de Sarrià – today a mix of old and new, with a sprinkling of shops and restaurants. At its top end is pretty Plaça de Sarrià (from which Passeig de la Reina Elisenda de Montcada leads west to the medieval Museu-Monestir de Pedralbes). As you wander downhill, duck off into Plaça del Consell de la Vila, Plaça de Sant Vicenç de Sarrià and Carrer de Rocaberti, at the end of which is the Monestir de Santa Isabel with its neo-Gothic cloister. Built in 1886 to house Clarissa nuns, it was abandoned during the civil war and used as an air-raid shelter.

the World's Best Dessert (the 'Seven Textures of Chocolate') in 2001. In his chocolate gallery-cum-boutique it's all about exquisite, finely crafted chocolate collections and cakes. After a visit here, you'll never want to buy ordinary chocolate again. (www.oriolbalaguer.com; Plaça de Sant Gregori Taumaturg 2; ☺10am-9pm Mon-Sat, to 2.30pm Sun; ⓇFGC La Bonanova)

The Best of
Barcelona

Antoni Gaudí's architectural creations in Park Güell
GÜNTER LENZ/IMAGEBROKER ©

Best Walks
The Old City in a Day

🏃 The Walk

The triptych of El Raval, the Barri Gòtic and La Ribera is where Barcelona was born. La Ribera, with El Born, is quintessential Barcelona – an icon of cool but still home to attractions of more enduring progeny. The Barri Gòtic is the old city's heart and soul, while El Raval isn't so much pulling itself up by its bootstraps as changing its boots for a pair of Manolo Blahniks. This walk takes you through these areas, past fabulous museums, monuments to antiquity, irresistible La Rambla and intimate little squares en route.

Start Museu Picasso; Ⓜ Jaume I

Finish Museu d'Art Contemporani de Barcelona; Ⓜ Universitat

Length 1.5km; one hour

🍴 Take a Break

Art deco and bohemian, **Cafè de L'Òpera** (p37) has had a front-row seat on La Rambla since 1929 and is the perfect old-city rest stop.

Gothic courtyard in Museu Picasso

❶ Museu Picasso

The **Museu Picasso** (p56) is best visited early in the morning, making it the ideal place to begin your walk. Apart from the early Picasso paintings that so distinguish this museum, the medieval mansions that make up the gallery have been beautifully preserved.

❷ Església de Santa Maria del Mar

Carrer de Montcada, a typical old-city lane – narrow, boisterous and leading somewhere interesting – passes some fine tapas bars, then emerges at the lovely, shaded Passeig del Born (on your left) with the **Església de Santa Maria del Mar** (p58) on your right. A pinnacle of Catalan Gothic, this church is all grace, light and elegance within.

❸ La Catedral

Out the church's south-west door, the Plaça de Santa Maria del Mar is a lovely little square, from which pedestrianised Carrer de l'Argenteria leads northwest to the Barri Gòtic. Pass the

KRZYSZTOF DYDYNSKI/LONELY PLANET IMAGES ©

remnants of Roman walls, and continue on to the Gothic centrepiece of Barcelona's oldest quarter, **La Catedral** (p28), which is at once sombre and a gilded study in excess.

❹ Plaça de Sant Josep Oriol

Few squares punctuate the Barri Gòtic, but the **Plaça de Sant Josep Oriol** is filled with charm. Watched over by **Església de Santa Maria del Pi** (p34), ringed with old shops and bars, and home to painters and farmers markets on

Sundays, it's a place to linger.

❺ Plaça Reial

More lanes lead through the heart of the old city to the grandest of old Barcelona's squares, the **Plaça Reial** (p34), which is ringed by bars distinguished by lamp posts of early Gaudí vintage.

❻ La Rambla

La Rambla (p24) cuts through old Barcelona, transporting a river of people from L'Eixample to the sea. Walk north-

west through this tide of people and performers before launching off its western shore into El Raval.

❼ Museu d'Art Contemporani de Barcelona

Cutting-edge galleries are a Barcelona speciality, and the **Museu d'Art Contemporani de Barcelona** (p49) is one of the finest. Fusing a modern collection, stunning contemporary architecture and the shell of an ancient monastery, this place is Barcelona in a nutshell.

Best Walks
Modernista Barcelona

🏃 The Walk

The Modernista architecture personified by (but not restricted to) Antoni Gaudí is Barcelona's most eye-catching signature. You'll find examples rippling out across the city but it's L'Eixample that has the greatest concentration of Modernista buildings. With undulating facades, otherworldly interiors, playfully imaginative rooftops and nary a straight line in sight, Modernista L'Eixample is unlike any other cityscape on earth. This itinerary showcases why many visitors can't get enough of this breathtaking city.

Start Plaça de Catalunya; Ⓜ Catalunya

Finish La Sagrada Família; Ⓜ Sagrada Família

Length 3.5km; three hours

✗ Take a Break

Barcelona's tapas chefs are to contemporary cuisine what Gaudí was to early 20th-century architecture, and nowhere is this better exemplified than in **Tapaç 24** (p97).

① Casa Calvet

At L'Eixample's southern edge, Plaça de Catalunya is an important transport hub and good starting point. Northwest along Carrer de Casp, **Casa Calvet** (p97) is where Gaudí's love affair with Barcelona began in earnest. Sober compared to his later creations, this apartment block is sumptuous within.

② Casa Amatller

If Barcelona has a Champs Elysées equivalent, it's the Passeig de Gràcia, and close to its midpoint are some extraordinary Modernista caprices. **Casa Amatller** (p94), a masterpiece by Josep Puig i Cadafalch with echoes of gabled northern Europe, is one of the standouts.

③ Casa Batlló

You know you've arrived at **Casa Batlló** (p88) when you stumble upon dozens of passers-by gazing up at the facade with a mix of awe and amusement. Most visitors have the same reaction inside, where Gaudí turns the conception of interior space on its head.

Casa de les Punxes, designed by Josep Puig i Cadafalch

❹ La Pedrera

A little further up the hill along Passeig de Gràcia, **La Pedrera** (p86) is similarly adorned with a fine facade in the best Gaudí tradition. But it's the interior (the attic is like inhabiting a fossil, the apartment akin to inhabiting a dream) and the rooftop that transform this apartment building into the realm of genius.

❺ Palau del Baró Quadras

The Modernistas were inspired by everything from Gothic to Orientalist styles and you'll find all of these on show in the **Palau del Baró Quadras** (p97), close to where Passeig de Gràcia meets Avinguda Diagonal. It's the work of Puig i Cadafalch, a towering Modernista genius.

❻ Casa de les Punxes

Nowhere does the Modernista aesthetic intersect so clearly with the childlike evocation of a fairy tale than in Puig i Cadafalch's **Casa de les Punxes** (p97). Turrets resemble witches' hats

in this castle-like flight of neo-Gothic fancy.

❼ La Sagrada Família

Nothing compares to **La Sagrada Família** (p104). Gaudí's unfinished masterwork is quite simply one of the world's foremost architectural creations, at once the high point of the Modernista style and a work so utterly original as to deserve a category of its own.

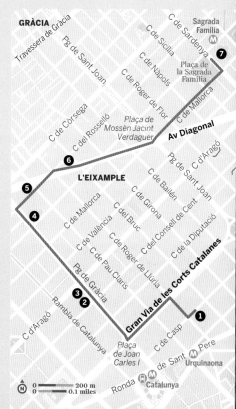

Best Walks
Food-Lovers' Barcelona

🏃 The Walk

Barcelona is synonymous with food of the highest quality and the ways to sample this are seemingly endless, from ageless tapas bars and Michelin-starred restaurants to roiling markets and corner shops that have been selling the finest local products for more than a century. Food in this city is a way of life, an entire subculture and one of the more pleasurable ways to enter into the local life of the city. This walk begins that process of initiation.

Start Quimet i Quimet; **M** Paral·lel

Finish Comerç 24; **M** Arc de Triomf

Length 3.5km; three to four hours

✕ Take a Break

You simply don't find places like **La Pineda** (p31) all that often any more, which makes this temple to traditional Catalan food culture such a treasure.

Mercat de la Boqueria

❶ Quimet i Quimet

Choosing our favourite tapas bar in a city world famous for them is no easy task, but **Quimet i Quimet** (p125) would always make the shortlist. Catalan tapas *par excellence,* bottles of every alcoholic beverage imaginable and an agreeable atmosphere built up over five generations are a near-perfect recipe.

❷ Granja Viader

Barcelona's tradition of milk bars finds its most famous expression in the timeless **Granja Viader** (p46) in El Raval. Its milk-chocolate drinks are renowned and the ambience is a cross between American diner and 19th-century Barcelona.

❸ Mercat de la Boqueria

Barcelona's best market, **Mercat de la Boqueria** (p44), is the most easily accessible of all Barcelona's culinary traditions. It's here that the city's celebrated chefs do their shopping, and it's all about colour, quality and people who take their food seriously.

❹ Escribà

Pastry shops are another essential pillar in the city's love affair with all things gastronomic, and a favourite example along La Rambla is **Escribà** (p41), offering pastries of every kind from behind its Modernista facade.

❺ Caelum

One peculiarity of Spanish cuisine is the food that emerges from convents all across the country. Many of these have been packaged up, along with other rare and artisan-made delicacies, and offered for sale at **Caelum** (p40). Stay long enough for a coffee in the medieval basement.

❻ Formatgeria La Seu

Barcelona offers numerous antidotes to fast food and **Formatgeria La Seu** (p41) is a wonderful shop window for farm-made cheeses made by small producers all across the country. The love affair with cheese is so obvious from the minute you step through the door that you'll quickly find

yourself thinking the same way.

❼ Comerç 24

Places like **Comerç 24** (p67) are the tip of Barcelona's culinary crescendo, taking recipes developed over

centuries of tradition and transforming them with that Barcelona penchant for innovation. It's chic, the proud owner of a Michelin star, and a wonderful place to rest at journey's end. Book ahead.

Best
Restaurants

Barcelona is one of Europe's richest culinary capitals and there are few corners of the city where you can't find highly regarded cuisine. Traditional Catalan is the mainstay, but there are also ultramodern designer temples to gastronomic experimentation and places serving dishes from the rest of Spain.

IMAGEBROKER ©

Barcelona's focal point may be avant-garde dining (think the foams and froths of master chef Ferran Adrià), but traditional cooking remains a foundation of the Catalan love affair with food. Fresh local ingredients are another touchstone of Barcelona's food culture. For the best tapas, see p148.

Rice

Grown in the Delta de l'Ebre in southern Catalonia, rice *(arròs)* features in many popular dishes. *Arròs a la cassola* or *arròs a la catalana* is Catalan paella, cooked in an earthenware pot without saffron, whereas *arròs negre* is cooked in cuttlefish ink. *Fideuà* is another passion; it's similar to paella but uses noodles rather than rice.

Sea & Mountains

Seafood features prominently on Catalan menus – restaurants in La Barceloneta serve little else – but meat from the Catalan interior also figures prominently. *Botifarra* (sausages) come in many shapes and sizes, and for some there's nothing better than a sizzling *solomillo* (sirloin) of *vedella* (beef) prepared *a punto* (medium rare).

Desserts

One dish dominates Barcelona dessert menus more than any other: *crema catalana,* a delicious version of crème brûlée.

Best Traditional Catalan

Agut A Barri Gòtic bastion of Catalan tradition with frogs' legs, *escalivada* (baked vegetables with anchovies), meat and seafood. (p35)

Ca L'Estevet Modern decor in El Raval with roasted meats, meatballs and homemade cannelloni. (p50)

L'Havana Another El Raval throwback with a fantastic *crema catalana*. (p51)

Pla de la Garsa Medieval setting with recipes from yesteryear, such as *botifarra* or salted cod. (p68)

Bodega La Sepúlveda A classic of old-school Catalan dishes such as cold meats, cheeses and chunks of fatty beef in gravy. (p100)

Sophisticated decor at Comerç 24

Best Seafood & Rice

El Passadís del Pep Well-kept local secret for the freshest seafood in Barcelona. (p67)

Can Solé A century of cooking seafood and some of Barcelona's best *fideus a banda* (noodles in a fish broth). (p81)

Cheriff Celebrated for its paella, which is usually brimful of seafood. (p81)

Suquet de l'Almirall Top-class seafood and rice dishes in La Barceloneta. (p79)

Best New-Wave

Cinc Sentits Michelin-starred and a laboratory for creative cookery. (p99)

Comerç 24 Another Michelin star, another showcase for delicious experimentation. (p67)

Espai Sucre Dessert oriented but sweet and salty in previously unimagined combinations. (p67)

Pla Old-style setting, new-style taste combinations with discernible roots in local traditions. (p35)

Somorrostro An outpost of original cooking in otherwise traditional La Barceloneta. (p81)

Best Setting

Torre d'Alta Mar Panoramic aerial views that take in the whole city. (p82)

Restaurant Casa Calvet Sophisticated dining with an extraordinary Gaudí interior. (p98)

Best
Shopping

A world-class shopping destination, Barcelona's sense of style pervades everything from fashion and home accessories to food shops, markets, antiques and handicrafts. Fashion's true home is L'Eixample and the streets surrounding the iconic Passeig de Gràcia. Elsewhere, boutiques in narrow old-city lanes feel like you've stumbled upon hidden treasure.

DIEGO LEZAMA/LONELY PLANET IMAGES ©

Fashion

You'll find boutiques devoted to the big Spanish designers alongside respected Catalan designers, such as the enduring Armand Basi and the celebrated and youthful Custo Dalmau. And there's barely an international brand that doesn't have outlets in Barcelona. The grid-like streets in the heart of L'Eixample – known as the Quadrat d'Or (Golden Square) – offer the richest pickings.

Food & Drink

Produce markets may grab the attention – the Mercat de la Boqueria could be Europe's finest – but Barcelona is also studded with little gourmet food stores, some unchanged in a century, others riding some new wave as is the Barcelona way. They're the perfect places to shop for a picnic or souvenirs.

Antiques & Homewares

Barcelona's old city – the Barri Gòtic, La Ribera and El Raval – are splendid places to set off on a treasure hunt, because it's in these twisting lanes that traditions survive, whether in the form of antiques, quirky local crafts or retro furnishings. At the other end of the spectrum there's Vinçon, Barcelona's cutting-edge purveyor of slick designer homewares in every imaginable form.

Best Fashion & Design Shops

Custo Barcelona Barcelona's most dynamic home-grown brand with outrageous cuts and colours. (p71)

Lurdes Bergada The tones may be more muted but this increasingly celebrated Barcelona designer is top-notch. (p91)

Armand Basi Women's fashions by a respected local designer who has been here from the beginning. (p91)

Vinçon The standard by which Catalan design is judged. (p90)

Camper Blending the casual with the classy, this world-famous Mallorcan shoe designer is consistently one step ahead of the market. (p102)

Designer fashion store Custo Barcelona

Bagués Where else could you find jewellery crafted into Modernista forms? (p91)

Best Food & Drink Shops

Mercat de la Boqueria Fresh food market and mother lode of Barcelona's culinary culture. (p44)

Caelum Sweets, preserves and convent-cooked cookies from all over Spain. (p40)

Formatgeria La Seu Farm cheeses from artisan producers throughout Spain in the Barri Gòtic. (p41)

Olisoliva Olive oils and vinegars from across the country in the Mercat de Santa Caterina. (p70)

Joan Murrià The finest products from Catalonia and elsewhere in Spain behind a L'Eixample Modernista facade. (p102)

Xampany Self-styled 'Cathedral of Cava', Catalonia's riposte to the dominance of French champagne. (p91)

Oriol Balaguer Some of the world's most extraordinary chocolates. (p135)

Worth a Trip
Barcelona's most authentic flea market, **Els Encants Vells** (www. encantsbcn.com, in Catalan; Plaça de les Glòries Catalanes; ⏰7am-6.45pm Mon, Wed, Fri & Sat; Ⓜ Glòries), northeast of L'Eixample, is where bargain-hunters rifle through everything from battered old shoes and bric-a-brac to antique furniture and new clothes. Go in the morning for the best choice.

Best
Tapas

Tapas, those bite-sized morsels of genius, are an essential pillar in Barcelona's culinary culture. Like all elements of Catalan cuisine, the breadth of choice when it comes to tapas is extraordinary, from the traditional Catalan way of serving seafood from a can to astonishing little taste combinations whose origins lie in a laboratory.

NEIL SETCHFIELD/LONELY PLANET IMAGES ©

The Truth about Tapas

Eating tapas in Barcelona involves discarding a few preconceived ideas. First, the success of the Basques in colonising the world with their *pintxos* (tapas) leads many to assume that the archetypal *pintxo* – two or three items perched atop a small piece of bread – is all you need to know about tapas. The Catalans know otherwise, and a more typical way of enjoying tapas is to order seafood from a can. Which leads us to the second misconception: in Catalonia, only the finest seafood is preserved in a can and is very often of higher quality than seafood served fresh.

Tapas Culture

Yes, you'll find tapas bars filled on any night of the week, but unlike in Madrid, San Sebastián and elsewhere, the real Barcelona tapas tradition takes place on Sunday at lunchtime, often accompanied by a *vermut* (vermouth). Also unlike elsewhere, locals don't as a rule head out on a tapas crawl to sample the best that each has to offer; they usually prefer to linger for an hour or two, sampling a range of tapas and using it as an accompaniment to good conversation and time spent with friends.

☑ Top Tips

▶ Tapas is best enjoyed as a pre-dinner snack; trying to make a full meal out of it can prove expensive.

▶ In Basque tapas bars, each *pintxo* comes with a toothpick and payment is by the honour system; keep your toothpicks and present them for the final tally.

▶ The best accompaniment to Basque *pintxos* is a slightly tart Basque white wine, *txacolí*.

Mussels in a traditional tapas bar, El Raval

Best Traditional Tapas

Quimet i Quimet Seafood from a can, home-brew beer and fifth-generation hospitality. (p125)

El Xampanyet Swirls of anchovies and a timeless atmosphere. (p61)

La Pineda Homemade *vermut*, canned seafood, cured meats and time standing still. (p31)

Elisabets Unchanged in decades and good for Catalan *fuet* (sausage) or filled rolls. (p47)

Cal Pep Traditional with the occasional twist from this tapas haunt of long standing. (p61)

El Vaso de Oro Grilled prawns as they should be, in La Barceloneta. (p75)

Bar Mut Spans the full range of tradition (cured meats, seafood in a can) with a few tricks. (p98)

Casa Alfonso Museum-standard interiors and lovely baguettes. (p98)

Celler Cal Marino Wine bar serving good Catalan tapas. (p126)

Bar Tomàs Down-and-dirty bar with peerless *patates braves* (roast potatoes with spiced tomato sauce). (p133)

Best Designer Tapas

Tickets Catalan cooking's first family, the Adriàs, run this temple to good (and surprising) taste. (p126)

Tapaç 24 Riffs on traditional tapas varieties in a slick white L'Eixample basement. (p97)

Cata 1.81 The whole world is an inspiration for the tapas here. (p99)

Gouthier The ultimate tapa – the humble oyster – dominates Barcelona's first oyster bar. (p133)

La Llavor dels Orígens The focus in this stylish place is Catalan regional produce. (p67)

Bubó A pastry chef's eye for flavour adds a whole new dimension. (p61)

Best Regional Tapas

Centre Cultural Euskal Etxea Basque *pintxos* lined up along the bar three storeys high in El Born. (p61)

Bar del Pla Tapas from all over Spain take on new life and direction. (p61)

Best **Architecture**

Few cities are defined by their architecture to quite the same extent as Barcelona. The weird-and-wonderful undulations of Antoni Gaudí's creations are echoed in countless Modernista flights of fancy across the city. But Barcelona's architecture is a multidimensional story, which begins with Gothic grandeur and continues with a spirit of contemporary innovation that adds depth to this remarkable cityscape.

KRZYSZTOF DYDYNSKI/LONELY PLANET IMAGES ©

Gothic Barcelona

Barcelona is one of Europe's Gothic treasure chests, and it was largely from these jewels that the Modernistas took their inspiration. Catalan Gothic took its own course, with decoration used sparingly and Catalan builders championing breadth over height.

The Modernistas

Modernisme emerged in Barcelona during the 1880s, the city's belle époque. While the name suggests a rejection of the old, pioneers of the style actually delved deep into the past for inspiration, absorbed everything they could and then ripped up the rulebook. For many, Modernisme is synonymous with Gaudí (1852–1926), but he was by no means alone. Lluís Domènech i Montaner (1850–1923) and Josep Puig i Cadafalch (1867–1957) left a wealth of remarkable buildings across the city.

Contemporary Architecture

Barcelona's unrelenting openness to new ideas and the latest trends in art and design ensure local and international architects find fertile ground for adding daring new elements to the city's skyline.

Best Gothic Giants

Església de Santa Maria del Mar Arguably the high point of Catalan Gothic. (p58)

Museu Marítim In the former Gothic shipyards just off the seaward end of La Rambla. (p79)

Museu-Monestir de Pedralbes A 14th-century monastery with a superb three-level cloister. (p133)

Museu Picasso Rare surviving examples of Gothic mansions, now converted artfully into exhibition space. (p56)

La Catedral The old city's Gothic centrepiece, at once extravagant and sombre. (p28)

The illuminated surface of Torre Agbar, with La Sagrada Família in view

Best of Gaudí

La Sagrada Família Gaudí's unfinished symphony and the world's most original church building. (p104)

La Pedrera Showpiece Gaudí apartment building with an otherworldly roof. (p86)

Casa Batlló Passeig de Gràcia's most eye-catching facade, with an astonishing interior to match. (p88)

Palau Güell Recently reopened and a match for Gaudí's better-known works elsewhere. (p49)

Park Güell Gaudí's playfulness in full swing on a hill overlooking the city. (p110)

Best of the Modernista Rest

Palau de la Música Catalana by Lluís Domènech i Montaner Breathtaking La Ribera concert hall. (p64)

Casa Amatller by Josep Puig i Cadafalch Dutch-looking neighbour to Casa Batlló with gabled roof. (p94)

Hospital de la Santa Creu i Sant Pau by Lluís Domènech i Montaner Gilded pavilions north of La Sagrada Família. (p106)

Palau del Baró Quadras by Josep Puig i Cadafalch Stained-glass and neo-Gothic flourishes. (p97)

Worth a Trip

Barcelona's very own cucumber-shaped tower, Jean Nouvel's luminous **Torre Agbar** (www.torreagbar.com; Avinguda Diagonal 225; [M]Glòries) is the most daring addition to Barcelona's skyline since the first towers of La Sagrada Família went up. Only the foyer is accessible to casual visitors.

Best
Art & Design

NEIL SETCHFIELD/LONELY PLANET IMAGES ©

Barcelona has for centuries been a canvas for the great Spanish and Catalan artists of the age – its streets, squares, parks and of course galleries are littered with the signatures of artists past and present, famous and unknown. From Modernista sculptors, such as Josep Llimona, to international and home-grown stars, such as Roy Lichtenstein and Joan Miró, they've all left their mark.

Street Art

Since the return of democracy in the late 1970s, the town hall has not been shy about encouraging the placement of sometimes grandiose and often incomprehensible contemporary works in the city's public spaces. Reactions range from admiration to perplexity. Justly proud of its rich street-art heritage, the council has also created an extensive archive of it all at www.bcn.cat (click Art Públic, under La Ciutat/The City). The site is rich in description of hundreds of items scattered across the city, and includes commentary on the history of the city through its street art.

20th-Century Art

Two of the great names in 20th-century art – Pablo Picasso and Joan Miró – had strong ties to Barcelona, and both left considerable legacies in the city. Much of Picasso's early work is on show here, as is the most complete collection of Joan Miró's masterworks. Aside from these towering international figures, Barcelona has been a minor cauldron of activity, dominated by figures such as Antoni Tàpies (b 1923). Early in his career (from the mid-1940s onwards) he seemed keen on self-portraits, but also experimented with collage using materials from wood to rice.

☑ Top Tips

▶ To learn about some of the city's lesser-known private galleries, consider buying the **Artco Ticket** (see the boxed text, p97) which covers entry to six such collections.

Best 20th-Century Art & Design

Museu Picasso A journey through Picasso's work before cubism took over his life. (p56)

Fundació Joan Miró Joan Miró's portfolio, from his formative years to later works. (p118)

Fundació Antoni Tàpies A selection of Tàpies' works and contemporary art exhibitions. (p94)

Visitors entering CaixaForum

Museu Nacional d'Art de Catalunya (MNAC) Modern Catalan art on the 1st floor of Barcelona's premier art museum. (p114)

Museu d'Art Contemporani de Barcelona (MACBA) Fabulous rotating collection of local and international contemporary art. (p49)

Fundació Suñol Rich private collection of photography, sculpture and paintings (some by Picasso). (p97)

Centre de Cultura Contemporània de Barcelona (CCCB) High-class rotating exhibitions, often focusing on photography. (p49)

CaixaForum Dynamic artistic space in a beautifully converted Modernista building. (p122)

Museu del Modernisme Català Modernistas (including Gaudí) turn their attention to home furnishings. (p95)

Best Street Art

Barcelona Head Roy Lichtenstein's 1992 waterfront homage to Gaudí. (p78)

Homenatge a la Barceloneta Rebecca Horn's tribute to La Barceloneta's pre-Olympics waterfront culture. (p82)

Mosaïc de Miró The work of Barcelona's artistic icon adorns the footpath of La Rambla. (p26)

Gaudí's Lamp Posts One of Gaudí's earliest commissions in the Barri Gòtic's Plaça Reial. (p34)

Worth a Trip

Situated behind the bullring and close to Plaça Espanya, the **Parc de Joan Miró** (Carrer de Tarragona; M Tarragona) was created in the 1980s and is well worth the quick detour to see Miró's phallic sculpture titled *Dona i Ocell* (Woman and Bird).

Best
Parks & Beaches

The tight tangle of lanes that constitutes Barcelona's old town can feel claustrophobic at times. But once you move beyond, Barcelona opens up as a city of light and of space, its parks, gardens and long stretches of sand bequeathing the city an unmistakably Mediterranean air. Locals love nothing better than to immerse themselves in these open spaces.

DIEGO LEZAMA/LONELY PLANET IMAGES ©

Pretty Parks & Gardens

The patchwork of parks and gardens that encircle central Barcelona to the east, west and north are much-loved focal points for local life – the ideal settings for picnics and the place to stroll, free from traffic and mass tourism. Parc de la Ciutadella and Park Güell are perhaps the best-known stands of green, but Montjuïc, on the steep rise that overlooks Barcelona from the west, offers the greatest variety for those looking to escape the noise of city life.

Beautiful Beaches

Barcelona's love affair with the sea began in earnest in 1992, when the development accompanying the Olympics transformed its waterfront into a sophisticated promenade. Thankfully, not all of what went before was lost and La Barceloneta retains elements of its one-time knockabout personality. It's a neighbourhood that combines those Mediterranean ideals of wonderful seafood, agreeable surrounds and a beach always close at hand. Yes, there are more beautiful beaches further along the coast, but Barcelona's city beaches are transformed by one simple fact: most lie within walking distance of a city the world has come to love.

☑ Top Tips

▶ Shop for your picnic at Mercat de Santa Caterina (p64) en route to Parc de la Ciutadella.

▶ Ditto at Mercat de la Boqueria (p44) on the way to the gardens of Montjuïc.

▶ Avoid overpriced eateries inside Park Güell – bring your own food here too.

Best Parks & Gardens

Park Güell Everybody's favourite public park, where zany Gaudí flourishes meet landscape gardening. (p110)

Parc de la Ciutadella Home to parliament, a zoo, public art and abundant shade. (p64)

Surfer on Platja de Nova Icària

Jardins de Mossèn Cinto de Verdaguer
Gentle, sloping Montjuïc gardens devoted to bulbs and water lilies. (p123)

Jardí Botànic
More than 40,000 plants faithful to a loosely defined Mediterranean theme. (p125)

Jardins de Mossèn Costa i Llobera
An exotic stand of tropical and desert flora. (p123)

Jardins del Mirador
Good views and a handful of snack bars below the castle. (p123)

Best Beaches

Platja de Nova Icària
Perhaps the loveliest of Barcelona's city beaches, just beyond Port Olímpic. (p75)

Platja de la Barceloneta
Plenty of sand and more of a locals' beach than others. (p75)

Platja de Sant Sebastià
Family-friendly beach where Barceloneta meets the sea. (p75)

Worth a Trip
The five beaches stretching northeast from Port Olímpic (starting with Platja de Nova Icària, followed by the Platja de Bogatell) have nicer sand and cleaner water. All have at least one *chiringuito* – snacks and drinks bars that are often open until 1am (Easter to October).

Best
Sports & Activities

MARK AVELLINO/LONELY PLANET IMAGES ©

Football has the status of religion in Barcelona. Indeed, in this traditionally rose-tinged town, one is tempted to see the Camp Nou football stadium as the principal temple of worship. The object of such ecstasy is Football Club Barcelona, one of the most exciting teams in Europe and a bastion of Catalan identity.

It all began on 29 November 1899, when Swiss Hans Gamper founded FC Barcelona (Barça). His choice of club colours – the blue and maroon of his home town, Winterthur – has stuck. By 1910 FC Barcelona was the premier club in a rapidly growing league. Back then, Barça had 560 members who were all chuffed at the team's victory at that year's national championship. Barça – now with around 156,000 members – is one of only three teams (Real Madrid and Athletic de Bilbao are the others) never to have been relegated to the second division.

Other sports rarely get a look in, but there are plenty of chances to go for a swim, including in the pool used for the 1992 Barcelona Olympics.

FC Barcelona match Watch Messi and co take on the world in a live game. (p131)

Camp Nou Stadium Tour Step on hallowed ground as you tour this epic stadium. (p131)

Museu del FC Barcelona A shrine to one of history's most successful sporting clubs. (p131)

FC Botiga Barcelona's club shop has endless Barça memorabilia. (p83)

Olympic laps Swim laps at the Piscines Bernat Picornell, the 1992 Olympic pool. (p122)

Poliesportiu Marítim Swim some laps, take a spa and enjoy a massage. (p83)

Port Olímpic Follow the waterfront to the former Olympic port, now a yacht marina. (p75)

Best
Views

Barcelona's position between sea and mountains makes for wonderful views, whether from terra firma or high above, aboard a cable car. Montjuïc and Park Güell offer multiple opportunities to look down upon this beautiful Mediterranean city, and there are lesser-known vantage points too. Tibidabo, on the highest hill (512m) north of the city, is reached by a combination of the FGC train to Avinguda Tibidabo from Catalunya station, Barcelona's last surviving tram and funicular, and has the best and most far-ranging views over Barcelona and out to the Mediterranean.

Best High-Altitude Views

Transbordador Aeri
Splendid views over the whole city and along the coast. (p78)

Bell Tower, La Sagrada Família A whole new perspective on Barcelona's most celebrated work in progress. (p106)

Park Güell Sweeping city views from the Turó del Calvari in the park's southwestern corner. (p110)

Mirador a Colom This monument surveys La Rambla, the old city and the waterfront. (p27)

Castell de Montjuïc
Fine views over the Montjuïc treetops to the city beyond. (p122)

Best for Iconic Barcelona

La Sagrada Família, floodlit Beautiful by day, luminous from dusk to midnight when floodlit. (p104)

La Vinya del Senyor
At night, wine in hand, beneath the floodlit church facade. (p68)

Park bench, La Rambla
Watch the endlessly fascinating passing parade of the world's peoples. (p24)

La Pedrera rooftop
Gaudí's fantastical chimney pots with stately Passeig de Gràcia behind. (p86)

Mercat de la Boqueria
The best views of the market are from the Museu de l'Eròtica. (p44)

Best
Museums

With such a rich heritage of art and architecture, few cities rival Barcelona's array of world-class museums. As always in Spain, the line between a museum and an art gallery is deliciously blurred; in this section we've concentrated on traditional museums that take you for a ride through the history of Catalonia and beyond, with detours into the world of art.

History Museums

You could easily spend weeks working your way through Barcelona's museums. At journey's end, if you've visited them all, you'll have been on an extraordinarily diverse journey through the history of Barcelona and wider Catalan region. The story of the layers of civilisation that have accumulated here, one atop the other, including the Jews and Romans, is a series of intriguing tales that add depth and context to your experience of the city. This being a port city *par excellence,* the story also leads further afield, with discourses on Barcelona's seafaring past that take in everything from Spain's former colonies to ethnological exhibits from cultures all across the world. From football to ceramics to civil war air-raid shelters, there's nowhere, it seems, that Barcelona's museums can't take you.

The History of Art

The arts loom large over so many aspects of Barcelona life, and the city's museums take up the story with aplomb. The breadth of subject matter is extraordinary, with modern architecture and Antoni Gaudí recurring themes. But where Barcelona's museums excel is in their preservation of Catalonia's unimaginably rich history of Romanesque art and architecture.

Best Journeys Through History

Museu d'Història de Barcelona Rich Roman ruins and Gothic architecture. (p34)

Museu d'Història de Catalunya A wonderfully composed ode to Catalan history. (p78)

Sinagoga Major A rare outpost of Jewish Barcelona. (p35)

Museu Marítim Barcelona as Mediterranean port city in the Gothic former shipyards. (p79)

Museu Barbier-Mueller d'Art Pre-Colombí Artefacts from pre-Columbian civilisations of Central and South America. (p64)

Museu del FC Barcelona All the glitter of the world's favourite football club. (p130)

CosmoCaixa science museum

Museu d'Arqueologia de Catalunya Catalonia's prehistory, Visigoths and Romans. (p123)

Museu Etnològic A typically international collection of items. (p125)

Refugi 307 Revisit wartime Barcelona in this evocative network of air-raid shelters. (p125)

Museu-Monestir de Pedralbes Window on monastic life and marvellous Gothic cloister. (p133)

Best Art History Museums

Museu Nacional d'Art de Catalunya Breathtaking Romanesque art and a peerless portfolio of Catalan artists. (p114)

Museu Frederic Marès Outstanding repository of Spanish sculpture, with Romanesque art the star. (p34)

Museu Gaudí Step inside Gaudí's mind and workshop with drawings and scale models. (p106)

Casa-Museu Gaudí Gaudí's one-time home in Park Güell. (p111)

Museu de Ceràmica Spanish ceramics in all their glory, including works by Miró and Picasso. (p133)

Worth a Trip

Kids (and many grown ups) can't resist the interactive displays and experiments in **CosmoCaixa** (www.obrasocial.lacaixa.es; adult/child/child under 6 & senior €3/2/free; ⏰10am-8pm Tue-Sun; 🚌60 or 🚃FGC Av Tibidabo), a bright, playful science museum housed in a Modernista building at the foot of the Tibidabo hill. Think fossils, physics and an Amazonian rainforest...

Best
For Kids

From street performers who strut their stuff the length of La Rambla to art and architecture that looks like it emerged from a child's imagination, the sheer theatre of Barcelona's streets is a source of endless fascination for kids. Throw in an abundance of child-centric attractions (including beaches, pools and parks) and this is one city that seems made for a family holiday.

RICHARD CUMMINS/LONELY PLANET IMAGES ©

Child-Friendly Culture

One of the great things about Barcelona is the inclusion of children in many apparently adult activities. Going out to eat or sipping a beer on a late summer evening at a *terraza* (terrace) needn't mean leaving children with minders. Locals take their kids out all the time and it's not unusual to see all ages, from toddlers to grandparents, enjoying the city until well into the night. A good starting point for what Barcelona has to offer for children can be found at www.kidsinbarcelona.com; its child-friendly listings are updated regularly.

Practical Matters

Most of the mid- and upper-range hotels in Barcelona can organise a babysitting service. Many hotels use **5 Serveis** (☏ 93 412 56 76; www.5serveis. com, in Spanish & Catalan), which you can also contact directly. It has multilingual babysitters *(canguros)*. **Tender Loving Canguros** (☏ 647 605989; www. tlcanguros.com) offers English-speaking babysitters for a minimum of three hours. Expect to pay at least €10 an hour plus a taxi fare home for the babysitter. If you're willing to let your kid share your bed, you won't incur a supplement in hotels. Extra beds usually (though not always) incur a €20 to €30 charge.

☑ Top Tips

▶ Ask for extra tapas in bars, such as olives or raw cut carrots.

▶ Adjust your children to Barcelona time (ie late nights), otherwise they'll miss half of what's worth seeing.

▶ Ask the local tourist office for the nearest children's playgrounds.

Best Kids' Attractions

L'Aquàrium One of Spain's best aquariums with a shark tunnel and 11,000 fish. (p78)

Beaches Plenty of sand and gentle waters within walking distance. (p75)

Zoo de Barcelona More than 400 species from geckos to gorillas. (p64)

Poble Espanyol A village in miniature that's guaranteed to capture the kids' attention. (p122)

Transbordador Aeri Exhilarating cable car that feels like a fairground ride. (p78)

Parc de la Ciutadella Central Barcelona's largest park with ample space to play. (p64)

L'Anella Olímpica & Estadi Olímpic Swim the same pool and walk the same turf as Olympic greats. (p122)

Camp Nou The football-mad kid will never forget a visit here. (p130)

Best Museums for Minors

Museu de Cera Typically disconcerting wax museum, complete with fairytale forest and time travel. (p27)

Museu Marítim All manner of model ships, rafts and tall tales of the sea. (p79)

Museu de la Xocolata Every kid's dream: a museum devoted to the ultimate indulgence. (p65)

Castell de Montjuïc Return to the Middle Ages and patrol the ramparts above the city. (p122)

Museu Olímpic i de l'Esport Kids who enjoy sport will never want to leave. (p123)

Best for Fertile Imaginations

Park Güell Fantastical shapes, animals in glittering colours and *Hansel and Gretel*–like gatehouses. (p110)

Casa Batlló Architecture made for kids. (p88)

La Sagrada Família Castle-like structure that seems to spring from a medieval legend. (p104)

Fundació Joan Miró Children can relate to the childlike shapes and strong colours. (p118)

Worth a Trip

For the Ferris-wheel ride of your life, head for the **Parc d'Atraccions** (www.tibidabo.cat; adult/child under 1.2m €25/9; ☉noon-11pm Wed-Sun; 🚆FGC Av Tibidabo, then 🚋Tramvia Blau & funicular), an old-fashioned fun fair high on the Tibidabo hill. Getting here's half the fun, but always check the website for opening times before setting out.

Best
Tours

Tours certainly aren't necessary to enjoy Barcelona, but a handful of tours can enhance your visit, either by providing you with an introduction to the city or by zeroing in on an important aspect of Barcelona life that you simply couldn't access or understand on your own. Self-guided tours are another way to delve more deeply into a particular area of interest, such as the Ruta del Modernisme (see the boxed text, p94).

KRZYSZTOF DYDYNSKI/LONELY PLANET IMAGES ©

Barcelona Walking Tours
(www.barcelonaturisme.com; Plaça de Catalunya; adult €11.70-17.55, child €4.70-6.30; Catalunya) The tourist office runs 17 themed walking tours that focus on the Barri Gòtic, Picasso's Barcelona, Modernisme and the city's food culture.

Cook & Taste
(www.cookandtaste.net; Carrer del Paradís 3; per person €60, market supplement €12; Ⓜ Jaume I) Fabulous English-language cooking classes, but expert 90-minute tours of the Mercat de la Boqueria can be added as a supplement (morning tours Tuesday to Saturday; evening tours Friday).

Bike Tours Barcelona
(www.biketoursbarcelona.com; per person €22; Ⓜ Jaume I) One of numerous operators offering three-hour tours of the Barri Gòtic, waterfront, La Sagrada Família and other Gaudí landmarks. Turn up outside the tourist office on Plaça de Sant Jaume; check the website for departure times.

Golondrina Excursion Boats
(www.lasgolondrinas.com; Moll de les Drassanes; adult/child/concession €14/5/11.50; ⏱10am-9pm; Ⓜ Drassanes) A seaborne perspective of the city with a 1½-hour jaunt around the harbour and along the beaches to the northeast tip of town. Shorter trips available.

GoCar (www.gocartours.es; Carrer de Freixures 23; per hour/day €35/99; ⏱9am-9pm; Ⓜ Jaume I) GPS-guided, two-seat, three-wheeled moped-cars with commentary as you zip around town. High on the novelty scale.

Best For Free

KRZYSZTOF DYDYNSKI/LONELY PLANET IMAGES ©

There are so many museums in Barcelona that seeing even a small proportion of them can seem like a major financial investment. But a series of combination tickets (see p175) help keep costs down, and some of Barcelona's top attractions charge no admission, while others have free periods, usually on Sundays.

Most government-run museums open their doors without charge on the first Sunday of every month. On other Sundays, most refrain from charging from 3pm to 8pm. And of course you pay no admission fee for attractions like markets, gardens and beaches.

☑ Top Tips

▶ Sometimes free entry is best avoided, such as at La Catedral (p28): during periods of free entry the sanctuary is overwhelmed with visitors. We recommend paying €5 and visiting in relative peace.

Best Always Free

Park Güell Public art at its most accessible; Barcelona's greatest bargain. (p110)

Església de Santa Maria del Mar Sublime Gothic masterpiece. (p58)

CaixaForum Art and architecture of the highest order: two for the price of none. (p122)

Fundació Fran Daurel Picasso, Miró, Barceló and more than 300 other works of art. (p122)

L'Anella Olímpica & Estadi Olímpic Relive unforgettable Olympic moments for nothing. (p122)

Temple Romà d'August Roman columns in old Barcelona. (p35)

Antic Hospital de la Santa Creu Wander unchallenged into grand Gothic reading rooms. (p50)

Best Free on Sundays

Museu Nacional d'Art de Catalunya Barcelona's top art collection, gratis. (p114)

Museu Picasso Picasso for nothing. (p56)

Museu d'Història de Barcelona Roman Barcelona without charge. (p34)

Museu d'Història de Catalunya Catalonia's historical story for free. (p78)

Església de Santa Maria del Pi Lovely old-city church; also free other days. (p34)

Best
Bars

NEIL SETCHFIELD/LONELY PLANET IMAGES ©

Bars proliferate across the city and Barcelona's bar culture is as diverse as the city itself. Bars are hubs of neighbourhood life. They are places to sample the region's highly regarded wines and *cavas* (Catalan sparkling wines), which have an understandably loyal following among locals. And bars are places that personify Barcelona's innate sophistication that seems nowhere more at home than in its wine and cocktail bars.

Bar Neighbourhoods

There are bars on just about every street corner in Barcelona, and every neighbourhood has its local watering hole. But the densest concentrations of dedicated drinking dens are to be found in El Raval, La Ribera (particularly El Born) and L'Eixample.

Neighbourhood Bars

Serving alcohol is only a small part in the role of a neighbourhood bar, and there are few better places in the city for witnessing unforgettable vignettes of Barcelona local life. Many bars open in the morning, in time for those on their way to work or for others taking a mid-morning coffee break. Late morning, the old timers sidle up to the bar, take up residence and often don't leave until some time in the afternoon. Next, it's the lunch crowd – any *barrio* bar worth its salt will serve food, either tapas at the bar or three-course lunch menus at a handful of tables out the back. Parents with kids on the way home from school, workers en route from work, evening punters preparing themselves for a big night – all make it their business to stop by their local bar.

Best Bars with History

London Bar Early 20th-century bar with Modernista interior and Picasso and Miró as past clients. (p52)

Casa Almirall Barcelona's oldest continuously functioning bar (1860) with wonderful period detail. (p52)

Bar Marsella They've seen it all at this gritty 19th-century El Raval bar. (p47)

Bar Muy Buenas A 19th-century classic with Modernista bar and multicultural leanings. (p52)

Les Gens Que J'Aime Romantic relic of 1960s L'Eixample with candle-light and red-velvet sofas. (p100)

The atmospheric interior of Bar Marsella

Barcelona Pipa Club
Fascinating former pipe-smokers' club with an air of cool conspiracy. (p37)

Best Neighbourhood Bars

El Vaso de Oro La Barceloneta as it used to be. (p75)

La Pineda A rare outpost of the old Barri Gòtic. (p31)

Raïm Old wine barrels, grizzled Gràcia locals and a Cuban love affair. (p109)

El Born Bar Long-standing local in dynamic El Born. (p61)

Best Cocktail Bars

Boadas Cocktail favourite of Hemingway and Miró. (p51)

Dry Martini Suited waiters and perfect dry martinis in L'Eixample. (p100)

Cactus Bar Sublime large *mojitos* in El Born. (p61)

Best Wine Bars

Bodega 1800 Choose from a long wine list in knowledgeable wine company. (p50)

La Vinya del Senyor More than 350 wines and a perfect setting. (p68)

Celler Cal Marino Wines by the glass and even take away. (p126)

Best Cava Bars

El Xampanyet Nowhere does the tapas-*cava* combination better than this 1930s-era El Born bar. (p61)

Can Paixano Ageless Barceloneta *cava* den of sheer, raucous pleasure. (p74)

Best Music Bars

Bar Pastís Shoebox-sized bar with music from French cabaret to tango. (p52)

Manchester Britpop from the 1980s and other UK classics. (p38)

Best
Cafes

Barcelona is distinguished by its historic cafes, where bow-tied waiters and period interiors are *de rigeur*. Many have been discovered by tourists, but you're still likely to find two men playing chess as they have done for decades, or a wizened old-timer, glass of cognac in hand, simply watching the world go by.

ANDREW PEACOCK/LONELY PLANET IMAGES ©

The Best of the Old

The Modernistas and others of their architectural ilk didn't content themselves with exotic facades. Just as often, the city's architects put as much effort into adorning the interiors of the city's salons. Such is the backdrop for many a Barcelona cafe. But in this city that seems hell-bent on redefining the future, it's the atmosphere in these cafes – the clientele and the decor – that serves to remind us that this is also a profoundly traditional city. Here, an older way of doing things prevails – a mid-morning coffee or something stronger, long hours spent solving the problems of the world with friends. And therein lies the *raison d'etre* of Barcelona's cafes: these are meeting places and hubs of social life, and have been for centuries.

In with the New

This being Barcelona, slick new cafes have also found a place in the affections of *barcelonins*. These are the sort of places where you sit beneath contemporary artworks as you update your Facebook profile to a soundtrack of lounge and other chill-out music, where the waiters are young and friendly, and where you're just as likely to encounter cocktails as coffee.

☑ Top Tips

▶ For sweet teeth, head for a *granja* (milk bar), where thick hot chocolate is the go.

▶ Don't take personally the gruff manner of old-school waiters. Believe it or not, it's part of their charm.

▶ A *café con leche* is a white coffee, *café solo* is a short black or espresso, while *café descafeinado* is decaf.

Best Historic Cafes

Cafè de L'Òpera The grand old art-deco dame of La Rambla, going strong since 1929. (p37)

Mauri Another from the class of 1929 with an

Inside Cafè de L'Òpera on La Rambla

ornate fresco and classy L'Eixample clientele. (p91)

Bar Velódromo Storied and wonderful L'Eixample cafe given a new lease on life. (p100).

Cafè del Centre Timeless cafe with old-style timber and marble, and a piano out the back. (p100)

Schilling Period decor, grumpy service and gay-friendly in the heart of the Barri Gòtic. (p38)

Best Hot Chocolate

Granja Viader Spain's most popular chocolate drink was invented in this 19th-century classic. (p47)

La Granja Leading candidate for Barcelona's best

coffee or hot chocolate in the Barri Gòtic. (p31)

Foix de Sarrià A 19th-century pastry shop in Sarrià with cakes and hot drinks for sampling. (p135)

Best Contemporary Cafes

Cosmo Archetypal modern art cafe – cool, chilled and creative coffees and teas. (p91)

Caelum Contemporary and historic, this is modern sophistication in a medieval Barri Gòtic basement. (p40)

Venus Delicatessen Breezy Barri Gòtic bar-cafe and a modern neighbourhood classic in the making. (p38)

Worth a Trip

French-run and as welcoming as could be, **La Nena** (Carrer de Ramon I Cajal 36; 9am-2pm & 4-10pm Mon-Sat, 10am-10pm Sun; M Fontana) does sinfully rich hot chocolate (known as *suïssos*), spongy desserts and savoury crepes. It has books all over the place and a kids' play area out back.

Best
Clubs

Barcelona's reputation as a party town is well deserved, although many of the better places are found in La Zona Alta, the upmarket suburbs north of the centre. If you can't move that far, there are options closer to the centre.

You'll find some fine clubbing in the Barri Gòtic, El Raval, L'Eixample and Montjuïc. Razzmatazz (www.salarazzmatazz.com; Carrer de Pamplona 88; admission €15-30; ☉1-6am Fri & Sat; Ⓜ Marina or Bogatell), seven blocks northwest of Port Olímpic, is worth the trip to experience five different clubs in one huge post-industrial space.

DIEGO LEZAMA/LONELY PLANET IMAGES ©

☑ Top Tips

▶ For nightlife info, source **Guía del Ocio** (www.guia delociobcn.es) from newsstands (€1).

▶ **What's On** (www. whatsonbcn.com), **Go Mag** (www.go -mag.com), **Le Cool** (http://barcelona. lecool.com) are also good.

Best Clubs

La Terrrazza Outdoor summer-only Montjuïc venue filled with top DJs and Barcelona's beautiful people. (p127)

Elephant Tents, gardens and a very cool crowd close to Camp Nou. (p134)

Moog Techno, electronica, retro pop and big-name DJs ensure a packed El Raval dance floor. (p52)

New York Best choice for a young crowd in the Barri Gòtic. (p39)

Antilla BCN Barcelona's premier club for salsa and sexy Cuban tunes. (p101)

Best After-Show Dancing

Bikini Latin, disco, hip-hop, funk...there's something for everyone at this stalwart. (p134)

Jamboree DJ-spun hip-hop and funk on Plaça Reial. (p39)

Sala Tarantos Flamenco till midnight, club dancing in the basement till dawn. (p40)

Bel-luna Jazz Club Danceable tunes from the '80s and '90s. (p102)

Sala Apolo House, techno and the like with an eclectic crowd. (p127)

Best
Gay & Lesbian

Barcelona has a busy gay scene and is one of the most gay-friendly cities in southern Europe. The bulk of the action happens in 'Gaixample', the five or six blocks of L'Eixample bounded by Gran Via de les Corts Catalanes, Carrer de Balmes, Carrer del Consell de Cent and Carrer de Casanova.

PETER SCHOLZ/CORBIS ©

Best Bars

Dietrich Gay Teatro Café Elegant setting and outrageous drag acts in this Gaixample classic. (p101)

La Chapelle Provocative religious decor and relaxed meeting place. (p101)

Best Clubs

Arena Madre (www.arenadisco.com; Carrer de Balmes 32; admission €6-12; ⊙12.30-6am; Ⓜ Passeig de Gràcia) Popular with a young gay crowd, Arena is one of the top clubs in town for boys seeking boys.

DBoy (www.dboyclub.com; Ronda de Sant Pere 19-21; ⊙midnight-6am Fri-Sun; Ⓜ Urquinaona) Once known as Salvation and a key club on the gay circuit.

Metro (www.metrodiscobcn.com; Carrer de Sepúlveda 185; ⊙midnight-5am Sun-Thu, midnight-6am Fri & Sat; Ⓜ Universitat) Both dance floors here are absolutely heaving on weekends with a 90% gay crowd.

Best Contacts

Antinous (www.antinouslibros.com, in Spanish; Carrer de Josep Anselm Clavé 6; ⊙11am-2pm & 5-8.30pm Mon-Fri, noon-2pm & 5-8.30pm Sat; Ⓜ Drassanes) Gay bookshop with a cafe.

GayBarcelona.com (www.gaybarcelona.com) Events, links and listings, including accommodation.

60by80 (www.60by80.com) Gay guide to the city.

☑ **Top Tips**

▶ Platja de Sant Miquel, south of La Barceloneta, is a gay-male nudist strip from mid-afternoon.

VisitBarcelonaGay.com (www.visitbarcelonagay.com) Another wide-ranging portal for gay Barcelona.

Worth a Trip

Sitges Half an hour southwest of Barcelona by train, this seaside party town is home to a huge international gay set from Easter to the end of summer. It comes to life again with a bang for *Carnaval* (Carnival) in February, when it hosts outrageous parades around town. For train timetables, check out www.renfe.es.

Best
Live Music &
Entertainment

Barcelona is an important stop for most musicians on any European tour. Above all, watch out for local band made good Ojos de Brujo (Wizard's Eyes), who meld flamenco and rumba with rap, ragga and electronica. But even the weekly diet of jazz, leavened with a little rock, flamenco and blues, keeps locals happy.

BARBARA VAN ZANTEN/LONELY PLANET IMAGES ©

Flamenco

As a general rule, Barcelona is only a middle-ranking flamenco stage. Where Barcelona has excelled, however, is in the peculiarly Barcelona phenomenon of Rumba Catalana. In the 1950s a new sound mixing flamenco with Latin (salsa and other South American dance flavours) emerged in *gitano* (gypsy) circles in Gràcia and the Barri Gòtic. By the late 1970s Rumba Catalana was out of steam, but new rumba bands have since emerged: watch out for Papawa, Barrio Negro and El Tío Carlos.

For more on flamenco in Barcelona, see www.flamencobarcelona.com (in Spanish).

Best Live Jazz & Other Music

Harlem Jazz Club One of Barcelona's most prestigious (and earthy) jazz stages. (p39)

Jamboree Another fine jazz venue that draws big names. (p39)

Bel-luna Jazz Club Good-quality jazz with nods to the blues. (p102)

Sala Apolo Alternative mix of offbeat rock acts, world music and DJs. (p127)

Plaça Nova *Sardana* (Catalan folk dancing) at noon most Sundays or 6pm Saturdays. (p31)

Best Flamenco

Sala Tarantos Good for a taste of the genre, with occasional big names. (p40)

Tablao de Carmen Touristy, but this is another good place to sample decent flamenco. (p127)

Best High Culture

Palau de la Música Catalana Modernista auditorium; everything from classical music to Spanish guitar. (p69)

Gran Teatre del Liceu World-class opera, an extravagant setting and fine acoustics. (p39)

Survival Guide

Survival Guide

Before You Go

When to Go

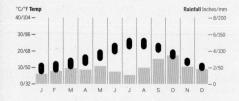

°C/°F **Temp**
40/104 —
30/86 —
20/68 —
10/50 —
0/32 —

Rainfall Inches/mm
— 8/200
— 6/150
— 4/100
— 2/50
— 0

J F M A M J J A S O N D

⇒ **Summer (Jun-Aug)**
Hot beach weather but often overwhelmed with visitors in July and August; locals escape the city in August.

⇒ **Autumn (Sep-Nov)**
September's one of the best months to visit; chance of rain in October and November.

⇒ **Winter (Dec-Feb)**
Nights can be chilly and there's a chance of rain, but there are few visitors and sunny days are possible.

⇒ **Spring (Mar-May)**
A lovely time to visit. Manageable visitor numbers, though rain is possible in April and May.

Book Your Stay

⇒ Accommodation in Barcelona is at a premium year-round so always book as far in advance as possible.

⇒ Barcelona's price to quality ratio is generally high, but prices can double on weekends, during important festivals and trade fairs.

⇒ Staying in the Barri Gòtic, El Raval or La Ribera puts you in the heart of the action, but nights can be noisy and long from Thursday through the weekend.

⇒ L'Eixample can be quieter, while La Barceloneta is perfect if you're here for the beach.

Useful Websites

Lonely Planet (www.lonely planet.com/spain/barcelona) Find recommended hotels and book online.

Splendia (www.splendia. com) Good for tracking

down some of the city's more striking hotels.

Barcelona Turisme
(www.barcelonaturisme.com) Tourist office with a booking service covering more than 300 places to stay.

Oh-Barcelona.Com
(www.oh-barcelona.com) More than 800 hotels and apartments to choose from.

Barcelona Online
(www.barcelona-on-line.es) Another decent booking engine.

Best Budget
Alberg Mare de Déu de Montserrat
(www.xanascat.cat) Hostel up the hill in Tibidabo set in a magnificent former mansion.

Hostal Campi (www.hostalcampi.com) Excellent, centrally located *hostal*; the best doubles have private bathrooms.

Pensió 2000 (www.pensio2000.com) Cheerful La Ribera *pensión* with canary-yellow rooms.

Hostel Mambo Tango (www.hostelmambotango.com) Fun international hostel with basic dorms in Poble Sec.

Alberg Hostel Itaca (www.itacahostel.com) Bright, quiet hostel near La Catedral with dorms, doubles and apartments.

Hotel Aneto (www.hotelaneto.com) Simple, good-value El Raval base.

Best Midrange
Hostal Goya (www.hostalgoya.com) A gem on the chichi side of L'Eixample with fine rooms and period features.

Hotel Banys Orientals (www.hotelbanysorientals.com) Boutique belle with beautifully designed rooms.

Hotel Constanza (www.hotelconstanza.com) A boutique hotel with lovely rooms and fine L'Eixample views from the roof terrace.

Hotel Neri (www.hotelneri.com) Stunningly renovated medieval mansion a stone's throw from La Rambla.

Hostal Gat Raval (www.gataccommodation.com) Colourful, hip, young, designer hostel deep in El Raval.

Chic & Basic (www.chicandbasic.com) Dazzling white rooms with a contemporary look in a historic building.

Best Top End
Casa Camper (www.casacamper.com) Gorgeous designer place run by the Mallorcan shoe people in the better end of El Raval.

W Barcelona (www.w-barcelona.com) Spinnaker-shaped glass tower at the end of a beach, with luxurious rooms and terrific views.

Hotel Omm (www.hotelomm.es) Ultra-modern rooms in a L'Eixample building with Modernista flourishes and a sophisticated foyer bar.

Hotel Casa Fuster (www.hotelcasafuster.com) Modernista mansion turned luxury hotel out of the scrum in Gràcia.

Best Short-Stay Apartments
Aparteasy (www.aparteasy.com) Excellent range of centrally located apartments ranking from small and dated to large and luxurious.

Feelathomebarcelona.com (www.feelathomebarcelona.com) Small, select group of apartments in La Rambla, El Raval and Sarrià.

Friendly Rentals (www. friendlyrentals.com) Dozens of high-quality options across the city from this experienced operator.

Rent a Flat in Barcelona (www. rentaflatinbarcelona.com) Flats near La Rambla, La Ribera, L'Eixample and elsewhere.

Arriving in Barcelona

Aeroport del Prat

☑ **Top Tip** For the best way to get to your accommodation, see p17.

➤ **A1 Aerobús** (one-way/ return €5.30/9.15; ☉6am-1am) from airport to Plaça de Catalunya (30 to 40 minutes) via Plaça d'Espanya and Gran Via de les Corts Catalanes every six to 15 minutes. Buy tickets on the bus or from machines at the airport.

➤ **R2 Nord train** (one-way €3.15; ☉5.42am-11.38pm) every half-hour from

airport via several stops to Estació de Sants (main train station, 20 minutes) and Passeig de Gràcia (25 to 30 minutes) in central Barcelona.

➤ A taxi to the centre (around 30 minutes, depending on traffic) costs €25 to €30.

Aeroport de Girona–Costa Brava

➤ **Barcelona Bus** (www. barcelonabus.com; one-way/ return €12/21; 70 minutes) runs hourly services to Barcelona's Estació Nord.

Getting Around

Metro

☑ **Best for...** Barcelona's Metro is almost always the best choice, with the most extensive network of lines and stations throughout the city. Exceptions include travel to Montjuïc and Sarrià.

➤ **Transports Metropolitans de Barcelona** (TMB; ☎010; www.tmb.net) runs a

Metro system with seven colour-coded lines.

➤ Single tickets, good for one journey no matter how many changes you have to make, cost €1.45 and can be bought at Metro stations.

➤ The Metro operates from 5am to midnight Sunday to Thursday, from 5am to 2am on Friday, and all night Saturday.

FGC

☑ **Best for...** Trips from Plaça de Catalunya to scattered attractions such as Tibidabo, Sarrià and Pedralbes.

➤ The **FGC** (www.fgc.net) suburban rail network goes numerous places that the Metro doesn't. It operates on a similar schedule and a one-way ticket costs €1.45.

Funicular

☑ **Best For...** Getting to and around Montjuïc.

➤ Cable cars connect La Barceloneta and Poble Sec with Montjuïc.

➤ The **Transbordador Aeri** (one-way/return €10/15; ☉11am-8pm) service runs from the Torre de Sant Sebastià (La Barceloneta) to Miramar (Montjuïc).

→ The funicular railway runs from the Paral·lel Metro stop to the Estació Parc Montjuïc and is part of the Metro ticketing system.

→ The **Telefèric de Montjuïc** (one-way/return €6.50/9.30; ☺10am-9pm) runs from the Estació Parc Montjuïc to the Castell de Montjuïc at the summit of Montjuïc.

Taxi

☑ **Best for...** Quick trips across town outside peak hour.

→ Taxis are reasonably priced and charges are posted on passenger-side windows inside. The trip from Plaça de Catalunya to Park Güell costs about €10.

→ You can call a **taxi** (☎93 225 00 00, 93 300 11 00, 93 303 30 33, 93 322 22 22) or flag one down in the street.

Bus

☑ **Best for...** Night trips and those for whom Metro stairs are impassable (people with prams, travellers with disabilities).

→ **TMB buses** (☎010; www.tmb.net) run from 5am or 6am to as late as 11pm, depending on

the line. Many routes pass through Plaça de Catalunya and/or Plaça de la Universitat.

→ After 11pm a reduced network of yellow *nitbusos* (night buses) runs until 3am or 5am. All *nitbus* routes pass through Plaça de Catalunya and most run every 30 to 45 minutes. Single tickets cost €1.45 and can be purchased on the bus.

Essential Information

Business Hours

Standard business hours are as follows, unless specified in the reviews:

Banks 8.30am-2pm Mon-Fri; some also 4-7pm Thu and 9am-1pm Sat

Tickets & Passes

Targetes are multiple-trip tickets, sold at most Metro stations, that will save you time and money. A T-10 ticket (€8.25) gives you 10 trips on the Metro, buses and FGC trains; a T-DIA (€6.20) gives unlimited travel on all transport for one day. Two-/three-/four-/five-day tickets for unlimited travel on all transport excluding Aerobús cost €11.50/16.50/21/25.

Central Post Offices 8.30am-9.30pm Mon-Fri, 8.30am-2pm Sat

Restaurants lunch 1-4pm, dinner 8pm-midnight

Shops 10am-2pm & 4.30-7.30pm or 5-8pm

Discount Cards

The following (except student cards) are available at tourist offices:

ArticketBCN See the boxed text, p49.

ArqueoTicket Entry to five museums (Museu Marítim, Museu d'Història de Barcelona, Museu d'Arqueologia de Catalunya, Museu Egipci and Museu Barbier-Mueller d'Art Pre-Colombí).

Artco Ticket See the boxed text, p97.

Barcelona Card (www.barcelonacard.com; 2/3/4/5 days €27/33/37.50/44.50)

Free transport (and 20% off the Aerobús) and discounted admission (up to 30% off) or free entry to many sights. Cheaper if you book online, and kids' versions are available.

Ruta del Modernisme
Discounts at Barcelona's main Modernista sights. See the boxed text, p94.

Student Cards Discounts of up to 50% at many sights.

Electricity

230V/50Hz

Emergency

➜ Ambulance ☎061

➜ EU Standard Emergency Number ☎112

➜ Fire ☎080 or 085

➜ Police (Mossos d'Esquadra) ☎088

Money

Currency Spain uses the euro.

ATMs Widely available; usually a charge on ATM cash withdrawals abroad.

Cash Banks and building societies offer the best rates; take your passport.

Credit & Debit Cards Accepted in most hotels, restaurants and shops. May need to show passport or other photo ID.

Public Holidays

Many shops will be closed and many attractions operate on reduced hours on the following dates:

New Year's Day 1 January

Epiphany 6 January

Good Friday Late March/April

Easter Monday Late March/April

Labour Day 1 May

Dilluns de Pasqua Grande (day after Pentecost Sunday) May/June

Feast of St John the Baptist 24 June

Feast of the Assumption 15 August

Catalonia's National Day 11 September

Festes de la Mercè 24 September

Spain's National Day 12 October

All Saints' Day 1 November

Constitution Day 6 December

Feast of the Immaculate Conception 8 December

Christmas Day 25 December

St Stephen's Day (Boxing Day) 26 December

Safe Travel

☑ **Top Tip** Stay well clear of the ball-and-three-cups (trileros) brigade on La Rambla. This is always a set-up and you will lose your money (and maybe have your pockets emptied as you watch the game).

Petty crime and theft, with tourists the prey of choice, is a problem in Barcelona, although most visitors encounter few problems. Take particular care on airport trains, the Metro (especially around stops popular with tourists) and La Rambla.

Telephone

Mobile Phones

Local SIM cards are widely available and can be used in European and Australian mobile phones. US travellers will need to set their phones to roaming, or buy a local mobile and SIM card.

Phone Codes

➡ International access code ☎ 00

➡ Spain country code ☎ 34

Useful Numbers

➡ International directory enquiries ☎ 11825

➡ International operator & reverse charges (collect): Europe ☎ 1008; outside Europe ☎ 1005

Tourist Information

The **Oficina d'Informació de Turisme de Barcelona** (www.barcelonaturisme. com) has offices around the city:

Money-Saving Tips

➡ Look out for free entry at sights (see p163).

➡ Order the *menú del día* for lunch in restaurants (see the boxed text, p38).

➡ Buy discount cards (p175).

➡ Buy 10-trip travel cards to get around the city (see the boxed text, p175).

Main Office (☎ 93 285 38 32; Plaça de Catalunya 17-S, underground; ⏱ 8.30am-8.30pm; Ⓜ Catalunya)

Aeroport del Prat (Terminals 1 & 2 arrivals halls; ⏱ 9am-9pm)

Barri Gòtic (Carrer de la Ciutat 2; ⏱ 8.30am-8.30pm Mon-Fri, 9am-7pm Sat, 9am-2pm Sun; Ⓜ Jaume I)

Estació de Sants (⏱ 8am-8pm; Ⓜ Sants Estació)

Travellers with Disabilities

Accessible Barcelona (www.accessiblebarcelona. com) Craig Grimes, a T6 paraplegic and traveller, created this Barcelona-

specific site; it's easily the most useful doorway into the city for travellers with disabilities.

Taxi Amic (☎ 93 420 80 88; www.terra.es/personal/ taxiamic, in Spanish) A specialised taxi service for those with disabilities.

Visas

EU & Schengen Countries No visa required.

Australia, Canada, Israel, Japan, New Zealand and the USA No visa required for tourist visits of up to 90 days.

Other Countries Check with a Spanish embassy or consulate.

Language

Both Catalan (*català*) and Spanish (more precisely known as *castellano*, or Castilian) have official language status in Catalonia. In Barcelona you'll hear as much Spanish as Catalan and you'll find that most locals will happily speak Spanish to you, especially once they realise you're a foreigner. In this chapter, we've provided you with some Spanish to get you started, as well as some Catalan basics at the end.

Just read our pronunciation guides as if they were English and you'll be understood. Note that (m/f) indicates masculine and feminine forms.

To enhance your trip with a phrasebook, visit **lonelyplanet.com**. Lonely Planet iPhone phrasebooks are available through the Apple App store.

Basics

Hello.
Hola.   o·la

Goodbye.
Adiós.   a·dyos

How are you?
¿Qué tal?   ke tal

Fine, thanks.
Bien, gracias.   byen gra·thyas

Please.
Por favor.   por fa·vor

Thank you.
Gracias.   gra·thyas

Excuse me.
Perdón.   per·don

Sorry.
Lo siento.   lo syen·to

Yes./No.
Sí./No.   see/no

Do you speak (English)?
¿Habla (inglés)?   a·bla (een·gles)

I (don't) understand.
Yo (no) entiendo.   yo (no) en·tyen·do

Eating & Drinking

I'm a vegetarian. (m/f)
Soy   soy
vegetariano/a.   ve·khe·ta·rya·no/a

Cheers!
¡Salud!   sa·loo

That was delicious!
¡Estaba   es·ta·ba
buenísimo!   bwe·nee·see·mo

Please bring the bill.
Por favor nos   por fa·vor nos
trae la cuenta.   tra·e la kwen·ta

I'd like ...
Quisiera ...   kee·sye·ra ...

a coffee   un café   oon ka·fe

a table   una mesa   oo·na me·sa
  for two   para dos   pa·ra dos

a wine   un vino   oon vee·no

two beers   dos   dos
                 cervezas   ther·ve·thas

Shopping

I'd like to buy ...
Quisiera   kee·sye·ra
comprar ...   kom·prar ...

May I look at it?
¿Puedo verlo?   pwe·do ver·lo

How much is it?
¿Cuánto cuesta?   kwan·to kwes·ta

That's too/very expensive.
Es muy caro.   es mooy ka·ro

Can you lower the price?
¿Podría bajar   po·dree·a ba·khar
un poco   oon po·ko
el precio?   el pre·thyo

Emergencies

Help!
Socorro!   so·ko·ro

Call a doctor!
Llame a   lya·me a oon
un médico!   me·dee·ko

Call the police!
Llame a   lya·me a
la policía!   la po·lee·thee·a

I'm lost. (m/f)
Estoy perdido/a.   es·toy per·dee·do/a

I'm ill. (m/f)
Estoy enfermo/a.   es·toy en·fer·mo/a

Where are the toilets?
¿Dónde están   don·de es·tan
los baños?   los ba·nyos

Time & Numbers

What time is it?
¿Qué hora es?   ke o·ra es

It's (10) o'clock.
Son (las diez).   son (las dyeth)

morning	mañana	ma·nya·na
afternoon	tarde	tar·de
evening	noche	no·che
yesterday	ayer	a·yer
today	hoy	oy
tomorrow	mañana	ma·nya·na

1	uno	oo·no
2	dos	dos
3	tres	tres
4	cuatro	kwa·tro
5	cinco	theen·ko
6	seis	seys
7	siete	sye·te
8	ocho	o·cho
9	nueve	nwe·ve
10	diez	dyeth

Transport & Directions

Where's ...?
¿Dónde está ...?   don·de es·ta ...

What's the address?
¿Cuál es la   kwal es la
dirección?   dee·rek·thyon

Can you show me (on the map)?
¿Me lo puede   me lo pwe·de
indicar   een·dee·kar
(en el mapa)?   (en el ma·pa)

I want to go to ...
Quisiera ir a ...   kee·sye·ra eer a ...

What time does it arrive/leave?
¿A qué hora   a ke o·ra
llega/sale?   lye·ga/sa·le

I want to get off here.
Quiero bajarme   kye·ro ba·khar·me
aquí.   a·kee

Catalan – Basics

Good morning.
Bon dia.   bon dee·a

Good afternoon.
Bona tarda.   bo·na tar·da

Good evening.
Bon vespre.   bon bes·pra

Goodbye.
Adéu.   a·the·oo

Please.
Sisplau.   sees·pla·oo

Thank you.
Gràcies.   gra·see·a

You're welcome.
De res.   de res

Excuse me.
Perdoni.   par·tho·nee

I'm sorry.
Ho sento.   oo sen·to

How are you?
Com estàs?   kom as·tas

Very well.
(Molt) Bé.   (mol) be

Behind the Scenes

Send Us Your Feedback

We love to hear from travellers – your comments help make our books better. We read every word, and we guarantee that your feedback goes straight to the authors. Visit **lonelyplanet.com/contact** to submit your updates and suggestions.

Note: We may edit, reproduce and incorporate your comments in Lonely Planet products such as guidebooks, websites and digital products, so let us know if you don't want your comments reproduced or your name acknowledged. For a copy of our privacy policy visit lonelyplanet.com/privacy.

Our Readers

Many thanks to the travellers who used the last edition and wrote to us with helpful hints, useful advice and interesting anecdotes: Valerie Davies, Steve Hoy, Deedee Koss, Andrea Warburton.

Anthony's Thanks

Huge thanks to Damien Simonis, whose work on *Barcelona* for Lonely Planet has been unrivalled. And special thanks to Marina, Carlota and Valentina who have made Spain a true place of the heart.

Acknowledgments

Cover photograph: View of Barcelona from Park Güell, Matilde Berk/Getty Images. Many of the images in this guide are available for licensing from Lonely Planet Images: www.lonelyplanetimages.com.

This Book

This 3rd edition of Lonely Planet's Barcelona Pocket guide was researched and written by Anthony Ham. The previous two editions were written by Damien Simonis.

This guidebook was commissioned in Lonely Planet's London office, and produced by the following:

Commissioning Editor Dora Whitaker **Coordinating Editor** Catherine Naghten **Assisting Editor** Carolyn Boicos **Coordinating Cartographer** Jennifer Johnston **Coordinating Layout Designer** Paul Iacono **Managing Editors** Bruce Evans, Anna Metcalfe **Managing Cartographers** Amanda Sierp, Diana Von Holdt **Managing Layout Designer** Jane Hart **Cover**

Research Naomi Parker **Internal Image Research** Aude Vauconsant **Language Content** Annelies Mertens **Thanks to** Laura Crawford, Janine Eberle, Ryan Evans, Liz Heynes, Laura Jane, David Kemp, Wayne Murphy, Trent Paton, Piers Pickard, Averil Robertson, Lachlan Ross, Michael Ruff, Julie Sheridan, Carlos Solarte, Laura Stansfeld, John Taufa, Gerard Walker, Clifton Wilkinson.

Index

See also separate subindexes for:

- Eating p190
- Drinking p191
- Entertainment p191
- Shopping p191

Our Writer

Anthony Ham

In 2001 Anthony fell irretrievably in love with Spain and returned a year later on a one-way ticket, with not a word of Spanish and knowing scarcely a person in the country. A decade later, he lives in Madrid with his Spanish wife, Marina, and their two daughters, speaks Spanish fluently and still adores just about everything about his adopted home. A regular visitor to Barcelona, he sometimes has to pinch himself to believe just how wonderfully life has turned out. When not writing for Lonely Planet, Anthony writes about and photographs Spain, Africa and the Middle East for newspapers and magazines around the world.

Published by Lonely Planet Publications Pty Ltd
ABN 36 005 607 983
3rd edition – May 2012
ISBN 978 1 74179 716 9
© Lonely Planet 2012   Photographs © as indicated 2012
10 9 8 7 6 5 4 3 2
Printed in China